The Kinderchat Guide to the Classroom

From the founders of #Kinderchat, this book provides a comprehensive, friendly guide to teaching in the early childhood classroom. Organized around the same core topics as #Kinderchat, conversational yet authoritative chapters cover everything a novice teacher needs to know, from setting up your classroom to establishing routines and engaging with parents. Learn how to effectively incorporate play, meet the needs of diverse learners, and cover curriculum like a pro. With helpful tips for working with a range of program structures, this is a must-have read for anyone new to the kindergarten or pre-K classroom.

Heidi Echternacht (@hechternacht) is cofounder of #Kinderchat, an online space for early childhood advocates and educators to collaborate. Heidi has been an educator for 20 years and currently teaches second grade in Princeton, NJ, USA.

Amy Murray (@happycampergirl) is cofounder of #Kinderchat and a speaker and trainer on learning through play, self-regulation, and behavior management. She is currently Principal of Early Childhood Education at the Calgary French & International School in Calgary, Canada.

The Kinderchat Guide to the Classroom

Heidi Echternacht and Amy Murray

NEW YORK AND LONDON

First published 2022
by Routledge
605 Third Avenue, New York, NY 10158

and by Routledge
2 Park Square, Milton Park, Abingdon, Oxon OX14 4RN

Routledge is an imprint of the Taylor & Francis Group, an informa business

Library of Congress Cataloging-in-Publication Data
A catalog record for this title has been requested

ISBN: 978-0-367-48164-3 (hbk)
ISBN: 978-0-367-46935-1 (pbk)
ISBN: 978-1-003-03834-4 (ebk)

Typeset in Palatino
by Newgen Publishing UK

Access the support materials: www.routledge.com/9780367469351

**For the #Kinderchat. We made a hashtag,
you made it a community.
For children, who have taught us more than we
could ever teach them.
For colleagues next door, across town and
across the world doing this work everyday,
we are with you.
And for our own parents, who let us be children, first.**

This means you!
♡ Amy

Contents

Figures

Images

Tables

Acknowledgments

The process of writing a book in 2020, while working full-time as educators through a global pandemic, would not have been possible without a great number of people who have encouraged, helped, cheered, and guided us through this process.

First, a book with "kinderchat" in the title must acknowledge the community that exists around that hashtag. If you have moderated, contributed, guest-starred, asked questions, or provided answers: thank you. If you are a college or university instructor who sends your pre-service teachers to our chat: thank you. If you have ever attended a weekly #kinderchat: thank you. If you have ever lurked on the hashtag, hoping to one day be brave enough to join the conversation: thank you, too (and please do join us when you are ready!). Specific thanks also to:

- Christine Lederer (@keeneelou), for taking on the scheduling and coordinating of topics and moderators this year, to allow us to somehow do our jobs and also write a book.
- Our 2019–20 and 2020–21 teams of weekly chat moderators:
  - Carrie Marshall (@carriemarshall1)
  - Mardelle Sauerborn (@learningmurd)
  - Rachael McDonald (@rachaelmcdonald)
  - Joel Seaman (@joelseaman)
  - Faige Meller (@dubioseducator)
  - Kerensa Smith (@learnwithkerensa)
  - Kathleen Ruff (@mmekathleen)
  - Meg Sexton (@teachermeg)

As promised, our overwhelming gratitude to our pal Lisa Murphy (@ooeygooeylady), for holding our hands through the process of receiving, understanding, negotiating, and accepting a contract to write AN ACTUAL BOOK. Your professional generosity defies words, and we are so happy to call you our friend.

And finally, we find ourselves in the strange position of feeling compelled to thank each other. For 13 months, we have taken turns bossing, cheering, encouraging, nagging, calming, questioning, and reassuring one another. While we have tackled this project in different, often opposite ways, it is better for having done it together.

Introduction and Getting Started

Who We Are

So, who are these two women who think they can tell you everything you need to know to be ready to teach young children? Amy and Heidi are career educators, with remarkably parallel paths from opposite sides of two different countries. We are both, and will always be, teachers of young children in our hearts, no matter our current job titles.

One fortuitous day in 2009, we "met" on Twitter, stumbling into a shared conversation about the unique realities of teaching kindergarten, and then discussing how the education chats and threads on social media were not meeting the needs of teachers of young children. The only logical solution: to start our own conversation. We made up a hashtag, chose a time slot, and #kinderchat was born.

We decided on the name #kinderchat because we wanted to be a kinder, nicer version of many of the educational chats out there, and also because *Kinder* means children in German. It was a surprise to us that after we started the #kinderchat hashtag, multiple grade level chats suddenly popped up. It was never our intention to be kindergarten specific but rather, to have our feet firmly planted in early childhood as a "children's chat."

Every Monday evening for the last ten years, as teachers of young children, we have gathered around the hashtag and talked with teachers from all over the world. This book was born not only out of our own experience, knowledge, and growth, but out of the wisdom shared so generously by #kinderchat participants over the last decade. We have been known to say "we just made a hashtag; you all made a community," and that is as true in these pages as it is every Monday night at 7 p.m. Mountain, 9 p.m. Eastern time. As you read this book, yes, you have Amy and Heidi in your corner, coaching you along, but you also have hundreds of the best, kindest, smartest, bravest, most brilliant teachers-of-young-children, all over the world cheering you along and sharing in the inevitable ups and downs that come with educating young children.

What We Believe

- That play is a practice, for both teachers and students. Think of it like a yoga practice, or a meditation practice: you do it, every day, because you believe it is important and good for you. Some days it is easy. Some days it takes work. Over time, it gets smoother and calmer and more natural. It makes you better. It makes you healthier. It is essential to your health, sanity, and well-being.
- That play is the most essential, powerful, and important part of children's growth, development, and learning.
- That young children are constantly learning. They are not always learning what adults intend them to learn, or what we think they should learn, but they are always learning. Always.
- That educators have an ethical responsibility to honor and consider children's development when we are facilitating their formal education.
- That the first years of formal schooling are critically important and utterly magical for both children and educators.

The Goals of This Book

It's easy to feel lonely when teaching young children and especially in kindergarten: many schools have only one kindergarten classroom and teacher, and teachers of other grades often think of kindergarten as a different world from "real" school. Whether you are a career fourth-grade teacher, suddenly thrown into this land of tiny furniture and sticky hands, or a brand new grad, skipping happily into your very first classroom, our hope is that this book will help you feel the opposite of lonely. We want this book to feel like having a wise and generous colleague down the hall, full of ideas, support, and much-needed humor. With this book on your desk, you have Heidi, Amy, and ten years' worth of #kinderchat brilliance at your fingertips.

We hope this book serves as a sort of "Bible" to teach kindergarten. Think of this as Julia Child's *Mastering the Art of French Cooking*, but for kindergarten – both involve spoons and a lot of guts, but we guarantee you will be able to make a "soufflé de crayon" by the end.

Any kindergarten teacher can tell you how not to follow a textbook of teaching methods or curriculum. We are frequently told kindergarten is "a little different." No, it's not different; *upper grades* are different. Kindergarten is the basic foundational age for schooling and can (and should!) serve as a model for all grades. We provide "step-by-step" methods to navigate your first year (or any year!) in one of the most difficult and rewarding teaching assignments out there: the kindergarten.

We want to stress that while we use kindergarten as a base reference and target for this book, you can use parts of this book as a general guide for teaching children from ages three to eight years old. While each age has its own unique developmental stages and needs, five- and six-year-olds serve as a midpoint of early childhood and often the first formal year of schooling; this forces the need to balance curricular requirements and developmental needs. This balance can also be adapted to other grade levels.

Kids on School: Monkey Bar Unit

We were spending a lot of extra time on the monkey bars one year as I noticed multiple kids in the class needed to strengthen their core and others didn't know how to "work" the monkey bars. Finally a child said, "Ms. Echternacht, we are in a monkey bar unit now, right?" Without missing a beat I replied, "Absolutely!" Even as a young child she knew school was about "units" and it made perfect sense to her that learning the monkey bars would be one.

Heidi

How to Use This Book

Just Keep Following the Rainbow

Each week we meet online, we feature a new topic led by our amazing moderators. We decided to "follow the rainbow" when creating a weekly rotating system to ensure we offered a consistent balance of topics and to remember whose week it was to moderate. This guide is arranged in that same format, with the idea that you revisit the colors over and over again.

Revisiting topics over and over again is critical practice for teaching. It's often tempting for teachers to pretend we know it all or have "mastered" a set of practices, when in fact our practices should be constantly evolving, changing, and adapting to new situations, research, and the unique circumstances of our class or school environment. Teaching is a lifelong course of study that is never finished. Whether you are new to teaching or an experienced educator, we hope that you will read and reread these pages to draw forth new inspiration each year.

The other reason we arranged topics by rainbow is as educators, we have each sat through endless professional developments on "reading" or "math." While those subjects are important to the practice of teaching, this approach limits the scope of the actual work of a child's learning. Music is foundational to reading and mathematics, as are art and play. These are the exact experiences that are often reduced and sucked out of early childhood programs in favor of more "rigorous" academic math and reading programs. Too often, teaching is presented as a black and white, when in fact it is full color. We hope we bring that world of color to you and ultimately, to children through the chapters of this book.

Getting Ready

It's July and you are starting to panic – you're not ready, you don't know where to start, and you're beginning to sweat while suddenly spending a lot of time on Pinterest. Have no fear, the #Kinderchat is here! Let's get started!

Mindset and Initial Research

A good place to start is learning what young children naturally like to DO. You should have had some experience with children by this point, hopefully! If not, spend as much time observing young children at play as you possibly can and read up on child development in the Yellow chapter of this guidebook. Observing children at play is critical practice and you need to log multiple hours "taking in" their developmental stages, quirks, needs, and tendencies. You can't go wrong when you are firmly grounded in child development! We have found that as educators with over 50 years of teaching experience between us, child development is one of our favorite and most essential topics. We see it often washed away after coursework in college to the detriment of programs and the ongoing practice of working with young children. Basing your classroom in developmentally appropriate practice is foundational to your practice.

Basic Philosophy

After reading up on the foundations of child development, look to the Green chapter on play as your guiding light. Play is the basis from which EVERYTHING will flow. From our perspective, we recommend that you literally plan little to nothing else for the entire first month of school besides playing and teaching basic routines. We outline this very carefully in the Red chapter, detailing the first day, week, and month of school. Do not feel pressure to achieve much of anything for the first month. It is better to go slowly and learn your class than to do a thousand crafts that distract you from getting to know who the children ARE as learners and friends. Establishing healthy, professional, robust relationships between students and teachers is the primary goal for teaching and learning; you are a child's introduction into the mysterious and wondrous world of "school."

Before we dive into the nitty-gritty of the chapters, we wanted to share some wisdom from one member of the Kinderchat. Christine Lederer is a recently retired, long-time kindergarten teacher from Alberta, Canada, who generously offered to share her tips for new teachers for inclusion in this book. You'll notice that much of her wisdom aligns with and supports the themes that structure our chapters:

Teaching Tips From Mrs. Lederer

Most of my thinking around teaching in the early years was – and is – formed by the work of the National Association for the Education of Young Children (NAEYC). Their standards and practices have always provided a foundation for how teaching and learning should look, sound, and feel. I also have been influenced by thoughtful colleagues, deep thinkers, and dedicated researchers.

With that in mind, here is a list of things to consider when teaching and learning alongside children of all ages.

Community and Curriculum

- Work together on creating a community – relation-ships built on respect.
- Keep the community at the heart of the learning – ask, "what is best for the child/children in this?"
- Listen carefully and ask the questions "what do you notice?", "what would happen if…?"

- Listen to the families, parents, and guardians. Invite parents into conversations.
- Think about the space you're in – is it inviting to all? Inclusive? Are there some noisy spots and some quiet spots? Can children find what they need?
- Pay attention to the curriculum (that's your job!), but filter it through children's voices, interests, and ideas
- Move! Encourage the physical!
- Sing! Even if you don't think you sing very well.
- Dance! See above.
- Laugh!

Teacher as a Learner and Learner as a Teacher

- Remember that you are a learner too – model that every day! With that in mind, be reflective and help your children learn to be reflective too. Ask questions like, "how do I/you know that?" and "what makes me/you say that?"
- Observe and listen to the children. Collect writing and drawing samples, pictures, paintings, audio and video clips. Watch development over time. Remember, it's a photo album, not a snapshot.
- Share and celebrate the growth of each child – regularly!

Setting Up the Classroom

After child development and play, the next important piece of "Getting Ready" is setting up your classroom. No, it's not making name tags or math folders, it's room *design*. Resist getting caught up in name tags (you won't use them) or placing decorations around the room. The LAYOUT of your classroom is EXTREMELY IMPORTANT. You are actually doing most of your teaching through the design of the room, which we explain in detail in the Green chapter: The Complexity of Play.

While you may enjoy room design, the less fun job that needs to be done at the beginning of each year is the arduous task of sorting through classroom materials: creating new kits and work bins, sorting through old broken or incomplete sets, cleaning out that closet you've been avoiding, making sure your craft area has enough yarn and your math manipulatives are clean and sorted properly. Choose one area to focus on and update each year and know it will never all be perfect at the same time!

Design 101: Creating Areas for Play and Exploration, How to Make the Room Work

In a perfect world, every kindergarten classroom would have:

- big windows.
- a sink.
- at least one entire wall with cabinets and counter space.
- lots of sturdy, flexible, easily movable furniture that provides lots of storage while minimizing visual clutter.

Knowing that most of us do not get to live in this ideal world, here are some key things to consider when setting up your room:

- Allow room for movement. Young children MOVE a lot (more on this in the Yellow chapter!), and teachers of young children also move a lot. Make sure there is room to safely walk from one area to another and to circulate between tables. A freshly set up classroom may look beautiful with all those little chairs tidily pushed in around the tables. Take a few minutes to pull all those chairs out at random angles, including moving a few to areas where chairs are not meant to be (this WILL happen, once the children arrive), and see if you can still walk without bruising the area from mid-shin to lower hip. If not: reconfigure.
- Reduce visual fatigue. Both adults and children feel more calm when our eyes are not drawn to a hundred different colors and textures at once. This is not about decor, but

rather about managing the amount of sensory engagement that your classroom demands before instruction even starts. Quick, easy, and (relatively) cheap ways to do this:

- If you have a choice, opt for natural or neutral-color furniture, with one accent color.
- If you inherit an assortment of mismatched furniture: paint or cover it with adhesive shelf paper so it is all the same neutral color, or group furniture of the same color together to help create cohesion.
- If you are asked whether you want carpet installed in the room, decline. Yes, you read that right. Having hard, washable flooring in the whole room will make the whole space more sanitary and flexible. You can use foam mats, area rugs, or bath mats to divide up the space and make some cozy areas.
- If you have bulletin boards, and you feel like you must cover them, consider paint or fabric (thrift stores carry flat sheets in neutral colors) rather than paper. If you must use paper, use flat, smooth paper rather than the expensive and wasteful corrugated rolls. Similarly, use plain-colored borders, or no borders, or the same print throughout the room, rather than having different busy printed borders for every season, theme, and holiday. (This also saves you money and time!) With some colored paper and creativity, you can also turn your bulletin boards into makeshift windows and morals.

Must-Have Centers

Knowing that every classroom and program is different, there are some key areas that every kindergarten classroom should have:

- An area for dramatic play: Ideally, this would include some play kitchen/house furniture and a dedicated table/chair setup. Failing that, this may be a box of toy dishes and food, and an assortment of costumes or accessories to encourage role play. With some creativity, you can also turn a table into a makeshift kitchen set by cutting out a few circles for oven burners, or find nice cardboard boxes to create a play stove and fridge.

- An area for construction play: children love to build stuff. To do this, they need room to sit on the floor and let their creations naturally expand. An easy guideline is that there should be enough open space for four children to stand with their arms extended and not touch each other. If you are cramped for space, your circle/meeting area can double as your construction center.
- An art area. A good art area has washable surfaces and is near a water source (most often the sink in the room; if you do not have a sink, put your art area near the door so water is as near as possible). If you can, include both horizontal and vertical drawing/painting surfaces. If you don't have (or don't have room for) an easel, is there a stretch of wall that could be covered in paper for drawing or painting?
- A quiet area. If you don't have room for a dedicated reading/library area, your quiet zone can include books, puzzles, and other low-key activities. Magnetic drawing boards (the most common brand is Magna Doodle) or individual whiteboards and markers are a good fit for this area, too.
- A group circle/meeting area. A key part of building a strong classroom community is having a space where the entire class can gather for stories, discussion, singing, and sharing. That said: this area takes up a lot of valuable real estate, especially in a small classroom! To make good use of this space throughout the day, it can double as space for construction, quiet activities, a picnic-style snack zone, or a gross motor area.

Materials

Every classroom should have:

- At least two kinds of construction materials, ideally a set of sturdy wooden blocks plus something in the Lego family. Generous quantities of both.

- A steady supply of drawing paper – all colors, weights, sizes.
- A steady supply of drawing materials – crayons, chalk, colored pencils. Markers are NOT necessary (see the next list!)
- A sensory table that works with wet or dry sensory materials. If you don't have room for a full sensory table, an underbed storage bin (with a lid), set on a regular table during playtime works great.
- A good-sized collection of picture books (we share our essential collection bins in the Orange chapter)
- A hundreds chart hung where students can see, touch, and interact with it.
- A box of versatile dress-up accessories and props for a variety of roles: hats, jewelry, shoes, bags, badges, gloves, aprons, and so on. Large squares of lightweight fabric in different colors can be made into capes, robes, skirts, wraps, and so on.

Things You Don't Need Even Though It Seems Crazy

- An interactive whiteboard (most commonly known as a "smartboard").
  For the cost of this, you can have a projector and a document camera, and spend the rest of the money on quality toys and manipulatives
- A premade calendar set.
- Posters with inspirational/funny sayings. Most of your students can't read yet, and after the first week, these will become invisible to you while still adding to the visual clutter.
- Materials themed to every season/holiday of the year. Don't waste your time making the same card game with apples, pumpkins, snowmen, hearts, flowers, and bunnies. Kids will enjoy the game and the learning no matter what shape the cards are.
- Markers. Really. Crayons or colored pencils are better for fine motor skill development. Save the markers for the occasional special project that needs them.

- To laminate anything. It's wasteful and usually unnecessary.
- A bunch of technology. Young learners are better served by real-life hands-on materials than by tablets or screens. We say this even after we endured remote learning. Having a few unattached keyboards around or a laptop they can collectively use and explore is fine.
- A fancy expensive rug for circle time. Children can sit on carpet sample squares, bath or yoga mats cut in half, dollar-store place mats, or even (gasp!) the bare floor.
- An alphabet hung above the black/white board. Hang it where kids can SEE it, use it, touch it, interact with it.

Setting Up a Classroom When You Have No Budget and No Money

If you are in a district or school that does not adequately fund your program, you will have to get creative. It's heartbreaking watching teachers have to crowdfund for basic teaching supplies or materials for their classroom, and we admit to feeling torn between wanting to help teachers and classrooms and being angry that teachers are asked to provide funding for their own workplaces. It is all of our jobs to help advocate for adequate funding for classrooms, and we hope this book gives the public more tools and foundations from which to advocate for funds for toys and kitchen sets.

That said, you can do a few things to cut costs (and be more friendly to the earth!):

- Create centers using everyday materials. Pull together string, clothespins, some doll clothes, two chairs, and, boom, you've got a play "laundry" area. (Bonus: add a washtub, water, and suds!)
- Use natural and found materials. You can do a lot with a stick and some sandpaper.
- Save nice cardboard boxes! A good cardboard box can be anything from a playhouse to a kitchen to a puppet theater to a container for math materials to a tray for a work space.

- Use outdoor space in new ways. For example: the humble mud kitchen. Schools in the UK LOVE the mud kitchen! It doubles as a sensory area and also a make pretend space. Outdoor "baking" with dirt and water? Yes, please!
- Spend wisely. Start small and buy the basics first. Basic white copy paper, tape, and some good crayons will go a long way.
- Use your local or school library. You don't need a class library, leveled or otherwise, which are very expensive to create. You just need to have a literacy-rich classroom with access to books. Create bins of books from your local or school library and return them as you add new titles and bins into the rotation.
- Ask for discounts everywhere you go. Whether it is the grocery store, an art supply shop, your local thrift shop, or a neighbor's garage sale, always ask (politely, of course!) if they offer (or would be willing to offer) a discount to teachers. You would be surprised at how many places are willing to do this, or even to donate the materials you need
- Go slow. Decide on one big purchase every year and slowly build your collection. It can take years to get a classroom put together, and no matter your funding circumstances, it's often better to build a program slowly and intentionally, rather than purchasing things you end up not wanting or using.
- Maintain perspective. The children's work is ultimately what makes a classroom. You don't need decorations; rather, you need to showcase the work of the children.

We hope this book serves you well throughout your career of teaching and learning with children. Each chapter is our collective experience of over 50 years in education. We remain curious learners each day and we hope you will too. It is a good and privileged life to live and work alongside the youngest of society's humans.

1

Red: Establishing Routines and Relationships

Too many teachers rush into curriculum before they've worked with their class to establish relationships and routines. No, we don't mean to write the "agreed-upon rules" or "good ideas of school" on a large piece of paper that everyone signs and no one looks at again. We mean doing the hard, exhausting work at the core of teaching far too many overlook. Your first full SIX WEEKS of "lesson planning" should be solely focused on establishing routines and relationships with your class. The hard work you do here will pay off in big dividends down the road. In this chapter, we show you how to slow down and make key investments in your class culture.

Routines: The First Six Weeks of Teaching

You will work harder in the first six weeks of kindergarten than you will all year long. Breathe that one in. Every ounce of work that you put into scaffolding structures and routines and building rapport with your class WILL PAY OFF. The key is to slow down, take your time, and acknowledge that *this is time well spent*.

- If you only do one thing for the first six weeks, it should be to actively build and facilitate relationships with and among your class.
- Your second goal is helping kids be independent in following school and class routines.
- Keep reminding yourself that **this is the general entire scope of your curriculum for A FULL SIX WEEKS.** Get to know your students and help them know each other and help them build independence in the classroom. That's it.

The First Day

To a little kid, whatever new grade they're entering, is like a baseball player's first time in the major leagues. This is doubly so for kindergarden. THEY ARE ABSOLUTELY, TOTALLY, AND COMPLETELY *STAR * STRUCK*. This is it, the big time, and they've hit it. They've been up and dressed since 5 a.m. They've dreamed of this moment every night over the summer and IT'S FINALLY HERE. It's all so exciting, it's possible they will literally *lose it at any moment*. To them, this is Disneyworld, Harry Potter Hogwarts, their birthday, and New Year's Eve all in one. This is kindergarten, baby. It's pure, raw, joy, and emotion, and you, the TEACHER, are the official ringleader.

If the first six weeks are tough, the first day of kindergarten is the toughest in many respects. If school starts at 8 a.m., be prepared to be *utterly exhausted* by 9:15. For this reason, keep the first day simple. Plan ONE THING and then cut it in half. The trick to the first day is surviving your first two hours. After that, you are primarily teaching the routine and holding everyone together until the end of the day.

Let's get clear here: we are going to tell you straight up that anyone pretending there's not a degree of desperation and complete and utter exhaustion in the first few days of teaching kindergarten for even the most experienced, kind, and capable teacher, is 100 percent lying to you via omission or inexperience. You will sweat, but you WILL GET THROUGH IT. Why desperation and exhaustion? Here's the first five minutes of the first day of kindergarten:

- José is crying.
- José's mom is crying.
- Petunia's grandma is picking her up at the car line early.
- Cara is going on the bus Tuesdays and Wednesdays, but not this week.
- Georg jumps into the room, trips, and starts crying.
- Sara knows Lola from camp and they are already BEST FRIENDS.
- Did you get Paola's allergy medicine? No tree nuts or dairy.
- Paula's allergic to peanuts and it's her birthday next week. Can she bring in cupcakes?
- Grace's mom would like to meet.
- Liam keeps touching the center you JUST SET UP.
- Jasmine HAS TO wear her glasses, which she hates. They're in her backpack. She thinks.
- Marcus can't find his cubby and is already eating his lunch.
- Marcus's mom wants to know if he needs sneakers today.
- The administrative assistant wants to know how many kids are buying lunch today and for you to have your attendance done by 7:55 a.m.

Meanwhile, YOU BARELY KNOW WHO IS WHO YET. And who the heck put Paula and Paola in the SAME CLASS?

Deal with the onslaught and chaos as gracefully as you can—it's important to be grounded and confident as you move around the room. **Everyone appreciates a teacher with a firm but loving hand** on the first day. You'll be sweating for sure, but *it's important you don't look flustered in the least.* It is all your pleasure, and everything is under control. YOU WILL BE OK. Just keep going!

- Take the time to greet every child (with eye contact and a genuinely warm greeting, of course!).
- Engage with parents. After a while, if you're having difficulty getting parents out of the room, get the class seated and start reading a book. Give a gentle= but firm, "Goodbye, parents! We will see you later today! We can't

wait to tell you all about it!" Let them lurk if they must, but you keep your focus completely on the kids. They are in your care now and you've got to firmly establish the classroom space and work on building rapport.

- A story works well to make the break from tearful parents or kids as it usually engages the children and everyone sort of knows the behaviors of "listening to a story," at least for the first few minutes of the first day. Keep the story short. There's a ton of "first day"-type books. Have a collection handy so you can read them throughout the first few days when you're desperate.

After your five-minute story, they will start wiggling. They've been so good. Did you notice? Say so! Brag them up! **Remember, they were working really hard during those first five minutes** because they are dying to engage! Did you know Petunia got a new backpack? Liam got NEW shoes! And José stopped crying, but now Sara wants to sit next to Cara and Lola's upset. Time to move.

The Importance of Props and Keeping It Moving

Jump up, hold hands, and sing a robust "Good Morning!" song. Sit back down. Get out your handy-dandy shiny object: a puppet, a literal shiny object, a rock, whatever it is, don't be proud, and talk to it. Oh yes, talk to it. They'll think you're a loony tune, but they'll be magically transfixed. Go with it.

Introduce yourself to the puppet, rock, whatever it is. A puppet is a bit more personal, but almost any interesting prop can work in a pinch. "Hi, Beavie the Beaver! My name is Ms. (Your Name)! I'm so glad to see you today!" You might even mention that Beavie is a bit shy to meet the new class and he's afraid he won't have any friends. Ask the kids if they'll be Beavie's friend and watch 'em melt.

Beavie's going to do a lot of work for you over the course of the year. Don't be too proud to bust out a puppet friend. You can project every insecurity you sense in the room onto this puppet friend. Model introducing yourself to Beavie with your name and favorite color, animal, whatever, and keep it moving around the circle until everyone has had a turn to share.

The prop often helps the quiet child open up, and if they don't want to contribute, you just say, "Marcus, would you tell Rocky the Rock your name later?" He'll nod thankfully. Always help a child save face. Give them extra time to gather their thoughts as it can often take them a bit longer to respond, but always be ready to rescue them quickly and gracefully.

Inevitably, someone will say, "I'm five!" and shock waves will roll through the crowd, "I'm five TOO!" Did you know they were five or six years old? They are! Get them back up moving with another game like "Head, Shoulders, Knees, and Toes" or whatever's in your arsenal. (We list a bunch at the end of this chapter!) Phew. You made it through the first 15 minutes! Time to visit the bathroom! It's new and different TOO! Get your play partner and let's go check it out!

Transition Times and Facilitating Relationships

- One helpful transitional routine to get students in the habit of, is to integrate frequent group bathroom breaks, water fountain, and cubby/backpack visits so all of your transition time is grouped together. This way you minimize interruptions during class time for bathroom and water breaks. Have students do their "three things" before going to recess, after recess, before and after lunch. Anytime there's a transition, give them some time and space to "take care of business."
- For the first few weeks of school, you can spend 15–20-minute intervals doing "three things" and you absolutely SHOULD! AT EVERY TRANSITION. By November, it will all be old hat, and while still interesting, they'll have a little dirt under their chin by then.

"Three Things":

1. Visit their cubby (very important for the first month of school, especially as kids need to spend A LOT of time talking about their backpack, lunchbox, or even just sitting and chatting in the cubby). Giving them TIME

to do this is not only soothing but also helps build community.
2. Use the bathroom. (Opportunity is knocking!)
3. Get drinks from the water fountain. (Yes, it's that exciting.)

Play Partners:

- Play partners help ensure that every child has the opportunity for some one-to-one time with each of their other classmates. You can be as strict or as loose about them as you need, but the general idea is that each child is assigned one classmate to line up with when you go places or they need a partner for something. Switch the partners up each day. You will quickly find it's the first thing they ask or remind you to do in the morning and a great talking point for parents and their children, "Who was your play partner today?"
- For a quick first day "activity," have play partners show each other their cubbies, backpacks, lunch bags, shoes, whatever they've got. If you're in a school where even one child might not have supplies, be sure to hand out a "school thing" so everyone can put something in their cubby and show it off and connect. It can be as simple a thing as a rock or pebble from your personal collection. It's not about the "things" as much as it is establishing the kids have THEIR OWN special place for THEIR things.

A Schedule for Security

For your first day, pretty much the only agenda you have is to make sure every kid has a good time. By this point in the day, the kids have been at school for 30–45 minutes. Believe it or not, they are starting to tap out. When is it time for lunch? When do we get to go home? Oh yes, we know it's 9:15 a.m. The schedule is critical to share that first day to help ease anxiety. We ALL like to know what's next and when "it" ends. Kids are no different. For the first day, keep it simple and try to chunk it all into five things. Use each finger on your hand to give them a visual. That way you can quickly switch to a nonverbal cue when Joey asks you for the bazillionth time when is it time to go home. Modify the following example as your schedule calls for:

- Thumb: "Good Morning" (all routines)
- Pointer: activity or going to visit places
- Tall man: lunch
- Ring finger: rest, activity, or going to visit places
- Pinky: play and snack
- Then it's time to wave goodbye:)

Save your ***ONE*** *VERY SIMPLE* planned activity for somewhere in the middle of your day. Any activity you plan should be a maximum of about 10–15 minutes. Honestly, the kids just really want to look at their lunchboxes, shoes, and look around at things and each other. Everything is new and shiny. Take the time to look around at things as a group. Spend the first day taking a walk to some of the places around the school they will need to go to, and greeting a few of the people they will see in the school. Practice doing "three things" and playing "getting to know you," simple nursery school-style songs, and clap games. Keep it moving!

In the afternoon, get outside and play. Like for all afternoon. This is how humans get to know one another, and children need LOTS of unstructured time to do that work. Make sure to have an extra afternoon snack and a rest time. Remember they've been up and PUMPED UP since 5 a.m. and they are pretty much toast after 11 a.m. that first day. A good rule of thumb for kindergarten is to plan for half days of an "academic" program and long afternoons of unstructured play.

Giving children the space to play and move, earns and builds trust between the teacher and the students. They are learning that they can depend on you to give them what they need.

A Note on Class Jobs

Jobs always feel very important at the beginning of the year and then seem to erode as the busyness of the year progresses. There are usually a few key jobs that are actually necessary to the class functioning, others that are highly sought after, and the rest are fluff. Some teachers incorporate jobs seamlessly into their day with great success. Class jobs can be a great way for children to take responsibility, feel ownership within the classroom, and help insure a daily routine. However, know that maintaining the daily routine of a job for everyone can get to be more of a headache than a help. It's OK to assign a daily job for the child who needs it and to let the rest fall to volunteering or being assigned as needs arise.

The First Week

Day two is a bit of a hangover for everyone, and the rest of the week is usually a complete blur. Everyone is coping with new sleep schedules and morning routines, still trying to find their way to school and back. Remember, *your primary goal is to get to know your class and to help them get to know each other.* For "math" and "reading," play whole-class games like "Jack Be Nimble" or "Punchanella," and incorporate "Ride and Read" as outlined in the Orange chapter into your routine. Get outside as much as you can. You don't need to do any formal academics the first week; rather, you need to observe and engage with your class and get them interacting with each other – that's it. If you are required to start formal academics right away, be sure to hand them a copy of this guidebook and work to incorporate these techniques as best you can.

By the end of the first week, your goal is to have taken your class through an entire week's schedule, slowly building in pieces of the routine day by day. The trick to teaching routines is to scaffold them in SLOWLY so that they help build both independence and confidence in your students to the point where, after six weeks of actual blood, sweat, and tears, you rarely, if ever, have to mention routines again. It becomes an invisible machine that *JUST WORKS*. In truth, so many teachers do this invisible work so well that most people have absolutely no idea how hard it is to do!

*Keep in mind, this work requires that you think through step-by-step how you are going to do *EVERY* THING**, which is again why we recommend not bothering with any "academic" work – *this IS the academic work*, helping children learn to self-regulate through their school day. Slow it all WAAAAY DOWN.

Even something as simple as having your class draw a picture requires thinking ahead:

- How will they choose their work space?
- What kind of paper will you use?
- Are you going to use this drawing in a portfolio?
- Do you have enough crayons for every table or child?
- What clean-up routines will you be reinforcing after they are finished working?
- What will the child who is finished in literally one minute do next?

Every routine or group behavior you want to encourage, brag up big time. "Oh, now look how nicely these two play partners lined up together, they knew just where to go!" Water fountain procedures: the child behind counts "3-2-1, NEXT" chant style, and, yes, they can get back in line. You are MAKING the time and creating the space. You will know you are on a roll when a new "routine song" spontaneously emerges from the collective. "Three things, line up at the gray wall" can turn into a kindergarten hip-hop favorite in no time.

Your ultimate aim is to establish a "community of kids" who have voice and choice in their classroom. The expectations you set help determine that culture. It's like its own mini society in some respects. To get it off the ground, keep things predictable but not rigid. The connection between the kids and you is more important than any routine. If you ever have to choose one, always choose fostering relationships over routines. By the end of the first week, every kid in your class should be feeling, "Oh yeah, I got this."

The First Month

It won't take long for challenging behaviors to emerge. One of the most endearing things about kindergartners is their transparency.

You will not need to guess how anyone is feeling or reacting! Part of the reason for taking so much time to establish your classroom routines is that it gives your kids a solid, predictable base of expectations from which they can operate.

By the end of the first month, hopefully they have tested you a bit. Any class worth their salt is going to test you a bit. Teaching and learning is a two-way street! While you are getting to know them, they are also checking YOU out! Oh yes, they are sly, but be assured your new little darlings are watching you LIKE A HAWK.

- Are you 100 percent consistent? Are you dependable?
- Are you sarcastic or terse when you talk to children, or are you genuine and kind?
- Do you listen to kids? Allow them to talk? Value their input?
- When you made a mistake, did you hide it? Own up to it? Model what to do?
- Have you built a relationship with EVERY CHILD?
- What essential routines have you dropped reinforcing?
- Can they depend on you to sense when they need to move?
- What did you do when someone told you "no" or pretended to not hear the direction?
- Might you be showing any favoritism? Where?
- Do you praise the way a child physically looks? (Don't!)
- How do you speak with your colleagues? Friendly? Or tense?
- Are you having fun, or are you projecting your frustration?
- When somebody did something "wrong," how did you react and what were the consequences?
- Are you fair?
- Are you trustworthy?
- Can they tell the difference between when you are serious about something and when you aren't?

By the end of the first month, you should be well on your way to communicating expectations to your class completely nonverbally. You've done the verbal praise, you've been consistent, and they should know the basics by now. A raised eyebrow or hand signal should go a long way. They like and look up to you, they trust you, and everyone wants to move forward to the next thing because *you've proved to them that it's way more fun to see what's next than to entertain themselves with poor behavior.*

That said, there are always years and kids that are particularly challenging, and we've all been there. Refer to the Blue chapter for more specifics on dealing with classroom management and behavior.

> *You will know what kind of year you're going to have the first time they help clean up the classroom. Do they work for the common good, or are they too busy with their own agenda or unaware of the team? If it's the latter, you're in for a long year.*
> *– Linda Rutherford, first-grade teacher, California*

By the end of the first month you should have:

- established a rapport with every child in your class.
- communicated positively at least once with every parent.
- established daily routines and a predictable schedule.
- made sure every child is aware of routines and working toward independence.
- a class that is beginning to function as a unit or team.
- made observations about each child and have some basic goals outlined.
- made sure every child has had individual time to play with every other child. (You'd be surprised at how many kids still don't know the name of their classmates even a month into school!)
- begun basic scaffolded reading and math activities as outlined in the Orange chapter.

Congratulations, You Made It!

The first six weeks of school are so tough because kids are testing you and you need to remain consistent in each and every interaction. Anyone who says that's easy, hasn't done it enough!

Being consistent is one of the most difficult aspects of teaching. Note there is a vast space between consistency and rigidity.

It seems like consistency would be the easy part, but reach back into your EdPsych classes and realize that you are actively shaping behavior. If you don't have your group in reasonable shape by this point, IT'S YOU, NOT THEM. That doesn't mean you don't have issues or problems with a particular child; rather, it means that by this point, you have your class humming along and working as a unit.

Young children expect and depend on routines and will hold you to them. Every teacher is familiar with the scenario where kids come into the classroom and within two seconds they have already asked, "Did you change the jobs yet?" Being consistent doesn't mean you never forget to change the jobs; instead, being consistent means they can depend on you to maintain the overall structure and include them when things change.

Rigid expectations, on the other hand, can damage your class, not only in fostering a class culture of "gotcha!", policing, and tattling, but ultimately the issue is that type of atmosphere results in children not building independence, self-regulation, and self-direction. Consistency fosters independence, while rigidity fosters compliance. By the end of the first six weeks, your class should feel like a joyful, safe, and happy place where everyone knows what to do.

Basics of Interacting With Young Children

- Little kids think THE TEACHER is all-seeing, all-knowing. Always remember, to them you hold massive amounts of power. Use and wield it wisely.
- ALWAYS help kids save face. They say they have read *Harry Potter* and *War and Peace* because they want to seem impressive and smart. Don't take that away from them.
- They want to feel and be safe, well liked, and to play, explore, and learn.
- They remember almost everything and yet can't remember anything. Keep multistep directions short and to the point.

- Sing as much as you possibly can. Music is magic.
- Puppets will do a lot of work for you. The kids "know" they aren't real, but are having waaaaaaay too much fun entertaining the fantasy, so don't spoil it for them.
- Kids can tackle big topics with astounding insight and will impress you with their kindness and generosity. They will also fight over who is sitting closer to the crayon basket.

The Importance of Observing

Whether you are highly experienced or just starting your journey working with children, observing kids at play and work is one of the most important things you can do as an educator. In addition to watching children in school settings, it is a key educational experience for teachers to observe children at play. Whether it be through babysitting, after school, or camp experience, observing a wide variety of children's developmental norms and processes is a powerful and necessary tool for any educator.

At the beginning of any year, observing children in your class should take anywhere from 30 percent to 50 percent of your attention. That may feel like a lot! When teaching young children, you will constantly feel pulled in 1,000 different directions at once. We guarantee you will never "get to it"– observation is something *you must prioritize.* Just put down the scissors, planbook, or conversation with a colleague and get to it. Recess and playground time is prime time to schedule into your day. Even then, it can be a challenge to ground yourself enough to stay still and live in the moment. Be aware that is where the children are living – in the moment. Observe that, marvel in it, and absorb the energy around you. After a while, begin to zero in on who is doing what, where, when, why, and how.

Your observations are a free and readily accessible assessment tool that is often underused in the classroom setting. Watching how children interact with one another both informs your practice and helps you learn more about each individual child. Observation helps you put your lessons in perspective. You worked three hours creating the perfect lesson and delivered it with razor-sharp perfection? They've already forgotten it and are now into crafting the perfect dandelion soup. Not that your lesson didn't matter or that they didn't learn, it's just that their SERIOUSNESS is right there – in that SECOND or MINUTE. It's that fast. And luckily, kids are forgiving of our best efforts.

Setting Up Class Rules and Management: Dos and Don'ts

We talk more specifically about classroom management, "rules" and behaviors in the Blue chapter. Please be sure to flip to that section and review, as classroom management and behavior is an ongoing, never-ending process. In the meantime, here are a few guidelines to get you going:

Relationships

The most fun thing about teaching should be the relationships you build with your students. And to be honest, it's harder work to do with some than others. It's your JOB to love each one of these kids, and if you can't muster outright love, you've got to at the very least achieve genuine appreciation. Usually, it's not the kids that are difficult to love; rather, it's a difficult parent or extenuating circumstance that can have you digging deep. Luckily, this is usually the exception. Kids and families, for the most part, are eager to learn, do well, and have fun.

Building Rapport Quickly

Learn their names, spell them right, pronounce them right, and USE THEM. Make sure to check with parents and kids about how they'd like their name pronounced. It can be difficult in passing to hear, focus, and get it all correct on a very busy first day, and it's extremely important that you get it right. This can be easier said than done as it can be a little awkward asking a parent to say the name again until you say it correctly, but stick with it

DO	DON'T
• Talk together about how rules help keep us safe.	• Have more than 3 "rules."
• Keep focused on achievable, age-appropriate, positive actions.	• Focus on the negative: "don't run in the hall, don't lick the floor."
• Spend a lot of time observing your class in unstructured play.	• Do any kind of big project before you've spent a lot of time observing children at play. This will help you spot potential pitfalls to your plans.
• Spend group time exchanging in dialogue with your class. Suspend your desire for an outcome or result, and just enjoy talking with them on any topic as if you are playing ball with them. Have frequent whole-group back and forth conversations.	• Waste time by making a long list of agreements, signing names to it, and then never using it again. Better to have no written rules than to create a useless document. Refer to the Blue chapter for specific guidance on how to create a class charter.
• Have a plan beforehand on how you are going to have them go places. Do they line up? Where? Try to keep it in the same place.	• Treat transitions as afterthoughts. Your "curriculum" for the first six weeks IS transitions. They are transitioning to school!
• Have a plan on how the students will move throughout the classroom. Realize that will ebb and flow as needs arise.	• Don't be surprised when children use the room in unintended ways. Stay willing and open to accepting their ideas. It's their room after all!
• Keep materials sparse and purposeful and add as needed.	• Don't overwhelm children with choices.

FIGURE 1.1
"Dos and don'ts" of establishing classroom routines

and have them e-mail you a pronunciation if you need to. Honor a child and family by showing that you are paying attention to what their child wants to be called in school.

Confession: Every year in the first few minutes of the first day of school – even after 20 years of teaching I think, "how on earth am I going to remember everyone's name?" I am terrible at remembering names, and oh help me when I have siblings I've had before. I've even misremembered kids' names as their mom's name. Yet somehow, I eventually remember and you will too. It helps writing them down a billion times while you're making your beginning-of-the-year lists and using their names frequently.

Heidi

Pro tip: **NEVER make all your name tags, cubby tags, birthday charts, and so on without parents first confirming their child's name and information.** *Every year it seems there are one or two spelling corrections to names. Start small with one name tag and have parents check the spelling, and THEN make all your cubby and name tags. It'll save you a lot of redoing.*

Nonverbal Communication Speaks Loudly

During the "great digital pivot" in the pandemic of 2020, everyone got a crash course on how important facial expressions are in engaging children. Teachers' facial muscles were sore from full-day workouts of overexaggerated expressions as we worked to engage children through computers! While digital engagement may require more extremes in this area, "in person" you'd be really surprised at how many people don't do this! Your facial expressions should be doing A LOT of work when you are around young children (and old people, too, for that matter!). Raise your eyebrows and say hello without actually saying ANYTHING! Look genuinely happy and interested to see people instead of the nonexpressive blasé face we often fade into in life. Nonverbal communication is so powerful and underused. Use it everywhere you go! Spread joy to old people on the street with a raised eyebrow and warm greeting. It's so worth it to see people's faces just absolutely light up.

I once had several lively and hours-long extensive conversations over a two-week period with a young child who only spoke Estonian and I only spoke English. The only word we repeated back and forth was "hello" and "keeshu- meow." We became good friends through literally hours and hours of sustained nonverbal conversation. We gave goodbye presents to one another. I found a whistle in a tourist shop and, without words, he gifted me a prized stick from his collection.

– Heidi

Facilitating Relationships Child-to-Child

One of the best ways to get to know the children is to help them get to know each other. That's what they are all there to do – make a friend. And they are each worried they won't have one.

Play Partner

Assigning daily partners for each child to play with can be such a comfort to the worried child. For the first few weeks of school, having play partners ask each other various questions and share together can help open up conversations and spark new friendships.

Show-and-Tell

There are teachers out there who love show-and-tell, but honestly, after a while it can get to be kind of a drag. However, KIDS ABSOLUTELY LOVE AND ADORE SHOW-AND-TELL. They want to talk to each other and show things to each other and ultimately PLAY WITH THOSE THINGS with each other. Don't be too proud to let show-and-tell shine. Switching it up from a whole-group activity to a partner share can help.

Activities and Games to Play as a Class

Some of our favorite games:

Oh yes, any game you play, you absolutely MUST do it 20 times over to make sure every child gets a turn. You'll hear it in your sleep, but that comes with the territory.

- Jack Be Nimble: Super easy, first-day stuff here. Use literally anything about the size of a candle and chant each child's name: "Cara Be Nimble, Cara Be Quick, Cara jump over the candlestick," and they jump over. This helps kids learn each other's names, and you can watch them puff up as they make the jump over the "candle."

- Punchinello: All the kids sing, "What can you do, Punchinello, funny fellow?" One child leads a trick in the center of the circle and all the kids sing back "We can do it too, Punchinello, funny fellow!" while they try it too. Good stuff.
- Head, Shoulders, Knees and Toes: A classic
- Variations of Stop and Go: Use nonverbal cues to indicate when they "freeze" or start to move again. As we discuss in the Orange chapter on curriculum, try it with symbols and road signs. Add in and use music to indicate the stop/start signals. At the "stop" portions, have them find their play partner and share a story or something about themselves, and then start the music again.
- Skip to My Lou: This can get a bit rowdy but it's a ton of fun! Especially with play partners. You can also mix up a pair and share with "Skip to My Lou" to keep it fun. When the song stops, pair and share! *This can also help you teach the procedure of what to do when you don't have a partner.*
- Circle dances: You can start with a basic "Ring Around the Rosie" to form the basis for multiple line, step, or square dances. Begin with the classic game and then vary using different songs and rhythms, utilizing clapping, differing steps, and motions. Try making both big and smaller circles. Moving together in various ways within a circle is powerful!

We urge you to play these games and other whole-group nursery rhyme types of games and to actively work to find new games to add to your repertoire. Sadly, many of these "old-fashioned" clap and movement games are disappearing from early childhood classrooms in favor of more academic activities. We can't stress enough how important these games are, not only to help you build community among children, but also because research supports that these types of games are very effective at helping children develop self-regulation skills – and that is ultimately what you are primarily doing as a teacher of young children. For more specifics on self-regulation and circle games, refer to the Yellow chapter on "Child Development."

Sources of movement, chant, call and response, and song games:

- *Raffi, Pete Seeger, Wee Sing, Ella Jenkins (a favorite!), Swingset Mamas, Red Grammer, and Ziggy Marley are a few classic places to start exploring. The world of children's music is huge! Look for new emerging artists!*
- *The Smithsonian Folkways website has a wonderful searchable database for wide varieties of culturally important children's songs from all over the world. Be sure to check it out!*

Interacting with Caregivers and Parents

Let's not kid around. This is the hardest part of the job of working with young children. Know that this aspect of the job gets MUCH easier as you gain more confidence and experience. It can be very intimidating talking to parents about their children when you are still new to the profession. Even seasoned teachers will say it's their least favorite part of the job!

For the most part, parents are your biggest supporters. It's really important that you view your role as being in actual partnership with parents versus seeing yourself as the provider of "parent education." That's a mistake we see even veteran teachers often make. It's an important distinction and perspective to adopt. While you, as a teacher, do have specialized knowledge of child development and curriculum, they have specialized knowledge of their child. *The parent-teacher relationship should always be one of exchange versus hierarchy.*

Your job is to meet each child and family where they are and to help them move forward in whatever way you can assist. For some families, that means helping parents see that little Marcus really CAN do it himself! For others, it means helping families get the support they need to ensure their child's safety and nutrition. Ultimately, you are there for *that child.* Think about what a really wonderful gift that is to busy families trying to juggle it all and worried if they are doing it right.

Parents are generally either super eager or semi-terrified about what you have to say about little Joey. Is he alright? Does he cry too much? He read *Harry Potter*, can you see he's clearly a genius? Does he have any friends? His older brother picks on him – is it affecting his work? Remember, parents are entrusting you with their heart each morning they send their child to you. Be gentle with them.

However, nothing can ruin a day like a difficult parent interaction. Here are our best tips for ensuring that you keep your interactions as positive as possible:

First Meeting

Be sure to smile and greet families warmly when you first meet them. Reach out and introduce yourself. Don't be shy! You are a professional! It gives everyone confidence when you have confidence! Keep your interaction light and short, and try to meet and greet every single family.

Back-to-School Night/Meet the Teacher

Every teacher dreads this night. Maybe there's one teacher out there in the universe who doesn't – if there is, we would love to hear from them! It's the one night you are stage front in the spotlight talking to a room full of adults who are all LOOKING YOU OVER. (No pressure!)

- Present yourself confidently and professionally.
- Overprepare!
- Tell them a little bit about yourself.
- Pause regularly throughout your presentation to take a nice long deep breath. You are likely speaking twice as fast as they are processing.
- If they laugh at your bad jokes, know you are in for a good year. If you get radio silence, smile and just keep going. It will be over before you know it!
- They *are* interested in curriculum, but they also know their kid is interested in their birthday and nervous about buying lunch. They know what's important to their child. Be sure you show them that you do too!

- If you don't know something, don't be afraid to say, "I don't know, I'll find out and get back to you!"
- Follow up via e-mail by sending out your entire presentation to everyone so that families that couldn't attend are included and can access the information without feeling awkward about asking.

One thing I've started doing at Back-to-School night is starting with the adults sharing out their memories of themselves in that grade. It helps to put things in perspective a bit. Kids don't remember the math curriculum, but as adults they can still remember how they felt thirty years ago when they felt picked on or excited about being chosen to erase the whiteboards.

Heidi

Conferences

Parent-teacher conferences may be the thing you dread but actually end up liking. You learn a lot about your families, which helps you get to know your students better. Getting to know a fuller picture of your students' family life and situation teaches you tons about each child.

Some schools even do home visits at the start of the year to help kids get acquainted with teachers. Having positive relationships with children's families and caregivers is as important as having positive relationships with the child. It's not always easy, but you definitely get better at it with practice.

Tips for Conferences:

- Overprepare as much as you can.
  - Have multiple work samples to share and discuss.
  - Be prepared to talk about academics, social skills, approach to work, and independence in school routines. Ideally, have anecdotes to share in each category.
- Be friendly, polite, and professional (which should go without saying by this point!).

- Let caregivers talk first – ask them what their child is talking about, what they say they like about school.
- Take notes when needed; often they are reminders to yourself to do something sparked by the conversation.
- Thank caregivers or parents for sharing and coming, and let them know you are there to help them and their child.
- Some will go more smoothly than others. Be prepared to be surprised!
- Have some music playing very softly in the background – it fills an awkward silence and can make you less nervous!
- If you have multiple conferences back-to-back over the course of an evening (or multiple evenings), have a system to keep things on schedule. The simplest is to have a polite note on your door, asking parents to knock when it is their time.
- Try to follow up with a note or e-mail thanking parents and reiterating any key points you discussed.

Earning Trust

It takes a while to earn trust among your new colleagues and families and establish yourself as part of the school community. And it should! Teaching is a very personal yet public relationship. Are you the teacher who is absent a lot? Out in public speaking poorly and loudly about your school or families? Teachers are entrusted with holding large parts of the community's privacy. Are you up to that challenge?

Tips for Earning Trust:

- Be predictable.
- Be fair.
- Be honest and transparent.
- Ask questions of colleagues before enacting new initiatives or major changes that may affect other teachers or classes.
- Communicate regularly (weekly newsletters, regular written or phone check-ins, and reply to e-mails promptly).

- Never share information about other students with another parent.
- Make sure your classroom, content, and curriculum represent all students and are diverse and equitable.
- Communicate any problems or issues quickly – don't wait, get ahead of it

Establishing Credibility When You Are New

There is usually a BUZZ in any school community about "the new teacher." You are getting looked over! There really is no community resource quite like a TEACHER. And now that's YOU! Kids, families, and colleagues are going to want to know all about you and can't wait to get to know you!

In addition to the other advice we've given here, the most critical piece for coming into a new school community is DO NOT TO GET SUCKED INTO SCHOOL GOSSIP with colleagues! Oftentimes the wrong players have been WAITING for new blood to come in so they can get more political players on "their side." Before you know the full picture of what's going on, you might find yourself aligned with what you eventually learn was the wrong end of town. It's important that for your first year – even your first few years – you stay focused on your classroom and try to keep the politics of the school community to a minimum. Work to build a diversity of relationships throughout your new school. You don't have to be a social butterfly, but you need to establish yourself as a professional.

The Formalities of School

Kindergarten has the special circumstance that it can be the *very first time* a family enters a formally structured school situation. They may have previously been in a drop-in day-care situation or a more casual home care arrangement. Many school routines are foreign to parents and caregivers. "School begins promptly at 8 a.m., with arrival times between 7:45 a.m. and 7:55 a.m., pick up is from 3:05 p.m.–3:30 p.m." might all be a new language to Harriet's parents who usually get her dressed around 10 a.m.

- Be patient – remember this is ALL NEW.
- Focus on one routine at a time.
- Use school resources such as nurses, counselors, and administrators to help you reinforce if needed.

Dealing with a Difficult Parent

Any server in any restaurant can tell you that sometimes people are just unreasonable. Well, those customers have kids and eventually one WILL end up in your class! Here's a few tips on dealing with very difficult parents:

- Be professional.
- Listen more than you talk.
- Repeat back "I hear you saying…, do I have this correct?"
- Communicate in writing so you have a record of your interactions.
- Be transparent, honest, and apologize and admit mistakes or misunderstandings.
- **Always** wait 24–36 hours to reply to an angry or tense e-mail. Give yourself some space and time to reply calmly and professionally.
- Recognize that ultimately it's not about you; it's about their life situation and/or their child. Do what you can and know the year will end! (We've ALL been there!)
- Ask for help from a guidance counselor, colleague, or administrator.
- Don't ever put yourself in a room alone with a hostile or angry parent.

Managing Expectations and Establishing Boundaries

Teaching is the kind of profession where you could work 24 hours every day and still feel like you're running behind. Between your colleagues, families, students, and administrators, you are always serving somebody! To stay centered in yourself, it helps to make lists and prioritize tasks. This is another reason why it is important to start your year off slowly and methodically so that you aren't frantically trying to deliver content and academics before the hard work of establishing and managing all of these relationships is solidified. Keep chipping away at it all bit by bit and it WILL all fall into place! We share our best tips and advice on this in the Violet chapter.

Assessment Checklist: Establishing Routines and Relationships

Use this checklist to help guide your thinking about each child in your class. It's not a "pass/fail" or even a "yes/no" checklist that you need to complete, but rather a list of things to think about in terms of how a child is approaching their first six weeks of school. Discuss with your students' caregivers and parents areas they excel at and where they could improve:

- has the tools and supports needed for success in school
- is well rested and ready for the day
- arrives on time to school
- follows classroom routines and multistep directions
- completes tasks in a timely manner
- makes transitions smoothly and respects boundaries
- cleans up and works as part of the class team
- plays well with others and makes friends
- is happy and interested in school
- resolves conflicts and solves problems appropriately
- feels secure about their social role within the class

References and Recommended Reading

Smithsonian Institution. (2020). *Smithsonian Folkways Recordings*. https://folkways.si.edu/search?query=Children%27s.

2

Orange: Curriculum

So your routines and relationship are coming along, but at some point you have to teach content, right?! Here's where you become the BOSS of differentiation and standards in kindergarten! Even if you are mandated to "cover" a curriculum that you know is not exactly developmentally appropriate, it is possible to cover all those pesky requirements while honoring the needs of five- and six-year-olds.

Inquiry Approach and Why It's Key

The inquiry approach will lead both YOU as well as your students to some of your most powerful learning experiences.

Children are by nature curious, excited, eager, and continuously zealous in exploring their surroundings. The two-year-old exclaiming, "why" at every turn, the four-year-old working to figure out "how" to work and create; each is exploring, asking, wondering, and assimilating new knowledge into patterns they've experienced, adapting that new bit into the old, continuously moving, growing, and changing. Kindergarten truly is the most wondrous occurrence of rapid learning humans will experience in their lifetime, most of which occurs without any "formal instruction," "exhibiting of listening behaviors," "assessments," or any of the jargon we place steadfastly necessary in the traditional role of "education."

Children don't care about "listening behaviors." They earnestly want to do well and be good, yes, but more importantly, they want to KNOW, they want to DRINK IT ALL IN, they want to taste it, hear it, see it, touch it, experience IT. They really don't want to hear you talk about whatever "IT" is for more than 30 seconds at a time. They want to INTERACT with you about IT. As adults hardened and trained by the world, it's honestly so refreshing a way to experience the wonder of life. Don't let yourself forget the wonder of it all!

It's tempting for an expert on anything to want to talk about THE THING. Taking an inquiry approach to teaching THE THING forces any expert to deconstruct the topic to allow an inquiry project to develop in ways you may never expect. Inquiry projects are lengthy ongoing pursuits of wonderings, research, and of sharing findings.

The inquiry approach takes continuous practice and discipline. It's not something that comes easily – especially in this time of busy lives and the feeling of content being so vast and urgent we just "download it" into students, assess them, and move on to the next download. Inquiry asks you and your students to co-create an experience, to enter into continuous conversation about THE THING. Ultimately, it's about helping children develop a relationship with learning, one that will hopefully be a joyous, continuous adventure.

Knowing What You Have to Teach

The essential starting point for your planning is knowing what you are required to teach. In the United States, this is most commonly referred to as *standards*, but in other locations or contexts, it can also be known as *learner outcomes*, *objectives*, or the *program of studies*. Whatever it is called in your situation, this refers to what you are legally responsible for teaching, and it is generally created by a government body of some sort. In many countries outside of the United States, the entire body of standards/

outcomes (for a given grade level or subject area, or for all grade levels/subject areas) is referred to as *the curriculum.* This stands in contrast to the American tendency to use "curriculum" to refer to packaged programs created by publishing companies and sold to schools/districts. For our purposes here:

- *Standard(s)* refers to the skills/knowledge/outcomes that students are expected to attain. These are mandatory.
- *Curriculum* or *program* refers to the lessons, activities, and projects that are undertaken in your classroom to help students meet those standards. This is where you may have some flexibility within the walls of your own classroom.

The most powerful thing you can do to equip yourself to offer a kindergarten program that aligns with your students' ages and needs is to be familiar with your standards. You may have a principal, or a district-mandated curriculum package, or a first-grade teacher down the hall, claiming that kindergarten students must be able to read by the end of the year, but **what do your standards say about that?**

"Ride and Read" Literacy

This beginning reading curriculum is intended for kindergarten-aged children. While it can be applied and modified for both younger and older learners, this particular outline is designed specifically for children aged between older four- and six-year-olds. Reading programs are too often dumbed down versions of literacy curricula designed for older children and don't honor the unique mind and spirit of a young child. Hopefully, this approach addresses that need while providing for the effective teaching of reading and writing.

- Step-by-step developmentally appropriate process shows you how to grow readers and writers of any level
- More than just letters/sounds

Note: If you have to "fill a requirement" of time in literacy, mix this approach with center time, drawing (writing), whole-class clap games, and read-alouds.

Ride and Read Scaffolded Skills Time Line:

- Basic: Stop/Go and Road Signs (weeks 1–3)
- Intermediate: Symbols and Motion Cards (weeks 2–4)
- Advanced: Wordless Books (start by weeks 3–4)

Ride and Read Supply List:

- Dry Erase Magnetic Color Labels www.5ssupply.com/product/dry-erase-magnetic-labels/
- Body Poetry: Animal Action Cards by Roylco https://roylco.com/shop/animal-action-cards/
- Let's Get Moving! Activity Mats by Lakeshore www.lakeshorelearning.com/products/active-play/balance-coordination/lets-get-moving-activity-mats/p/GG735

September and October: Establishing and Scaffolding the Progression of "Ride and Read"

Basic Ride and Read (weeks 1–3)

Objective: Your initial goal is to gain both leadership and the respect of the group, and to build trust, rapport, and classroom management skills while working to increase your group's ability to follow directions and maintain attention to tasks.

Materials

Materials: Road signs. You can make them, print them off the Internet, or order them through supply catalogues. Look for a wide variety of signs. In a pinch, you can just use red, yellow, and green construction paper circles to start.
Time: Implement this routine for ten minutes at a clip for about a week depending on your group.

- Use this beginning structure anywhere from one to three weeks depending on your group.

- Vary as needed and scaffold in complexity as each layer of the game begins to wear thin.
- Everyone learns to read on the first day of school by reading a "STOP" sign. Guess what, kids, YOU are now official readers! (*They are always* ***very grateful to you*** *for that declaration on the first day.*)

Meeting Time: Read and/or talk together about road signs for a few minutes before each daily session. They will have lots to share after they start looking for road signs!

Environmental print read-alouds like Tana Hoban's *I Read Signs* and then talk together:

- "What colors do you notice?"
- "What are the colors saying to the cars and people?"
- "Is there a pattern to road signs?"
- "Can we start to categorize them and put the colors together?"
- "Where else do you notice symbols that mean things?"

Color-coding reading:

Don't Tell Them What the Colors Mean; See If You Can Work Together to Discern a Pattern:

- Red signs mean: STOP! Look out! There might be danger!
- Yellow signs indicate: Go slow, watch out, be careful!
- Green means: GO! Play!
- Orange signs mean: Work!
- Blue signs indicate: Something special
- Black and white signs: Tell the rules of the road
- Brown signs: Nature, parks, points of interest

Activity: After talking about signs, it's time for the new readers to practice reading signs. Begin with basic STOP! and GO!, holding up red circles or stop signs, and green circles.

The children get in their pretend cars or saddle up their stallions or skateboards. Kids "read" when to STOP or GO! You control the flow with the signs. They are READERS now! And drivers! Utility!

> *NOTE: Some children will have difficulty stopping and waiting until the green light to start before moving. Stay playful, but also make sure you convey a certain seriousness when it's time to stop. If getting the group to stop is a problem, you're in for a long year.* **Stay in this practice until you both get it right.** *You will use the nonverbal skills and cues you develop right here all year long to help your class know when you mean business! Get good at it!*

This is classroom management 101. Practice this until it is an ingrained procedure and everyone is comfortable. It can get loud. Don't be afraid! Stop/Go and Loud/Quiet are good basic games for every early educator's repertoire.
Imagination and Rapport: Your ability to be playful while still maintaining control of the classroom will deeply resonate with children, helping you to build trust and establish rapport.

- As you gradually add in more signs as you talk about them in your read-aloud, the room slowly transforms into its own neighborhood with road signs placed all around the room. The children read the signs while riding their imaginary unicorns. "Speed limit 55! Go slow over there, there's a playground!"
- Add music – when the music stops, the children magically turn into statues. You are amazed and a little worried at this strange happening. "Oh no! Where did the children go? There are just these statues? Oh dear, what will their parents say!?" Luckily, just then, the music comes on, bringing them magically back to life and they are back to zooming on scooters. Adjust the stop and go times to help them slowly increase the practice of self-regulation.

Scaffolded Structures and Progression: Starting routines as pared down as possible while gradually scaffolding in structure helps children predict outcomes and expectations.

- Vary the game by adding in "find a partner" and ask them to tell each other their favorite a, b, c. This takes some scaffolding as kids will gravitate toward their friend and need help choosing other partners.
- Assigning rotating daily play partners can help structure this activity as you have partners discuss various topics. "Ask your partner what's their favorite … animal, color, game, and so on" with movement breaks between each question.
- Scaffolded skill building includes teaching children to raise their hand when they can't find a partner and having them find three different partners in a session. This serves as a precursor to the Reading Workshop "turn and tell" structure you might use during whole-group discussions as well as to eventual editing partners.
- Add motions to coincide with computer symbols for "mute" and "unmute"; hang up a phone, click a camera, pause, play, and so on for work on technology symbols reading.

Application: Use color-coding to create a schedule the children can read on the first day of school with their handy new decoding colors reading ability. This will also tremendously help those with the first-day jitters to be able to know when they can GO HOME or to get them through the day. Use dry erase magnetic labels color strips to indicate what's happening throughout the day, or you can make your own labels with construction paper. Start without writing words; just use the colors at first, then slowly add in words as your routine and schedule become more familiar.

Intermediate Ride and Read: (weeks 2–4, as needed)

Time: You should be able to sustain about a 15-minute reading practice activity session at this point.

Materials and Activities:

Symbology and Motion cards: Introduce these cards slowly in whole-group meeting sessions, followed by short activity sessions to practice building on the skills established in the basic Ride and Read model.

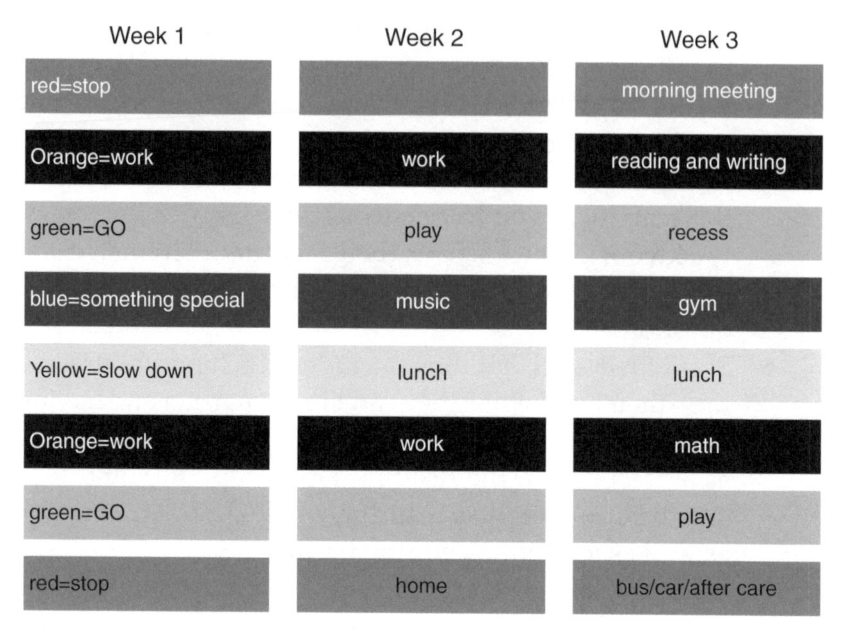

FIGURE 2.1
Color-coded schedule

- Animal position cards
  - Children read the animal position cards to determine the correct position of their body – make it match!
- Colored movement dots (math integration) and/or yoga cards
  - Place the cards around the room so the children go to a card or movement dot when it's time to STOP. They can then do that pose frozen or for an amount of movement (that is, ten jumping jacks or hold the position and count to 20).
- Explore, discover, and talk together about various pictures, signs, and symbols
  - This is where you introduce alphabet letter symbols (yes, the letter "n" is a symbol for a sound). Begin looking at the alphabet and the sound each letter represents. Use and incorporate alphabet cards into your Ride and Read time. ("Stop!" at the letter of your name and so on.)

- Go for walks and find signs around the school and building; look at computer coding symbols, math symbols, corporate logos, Asian writing characters, hieroglyphics; look at pieces of artwork; discuss remote learning symbols and tools.

BONUS: For a really good time, get yourself a couple of scooters (like the square ones they use in the gym) for your classroom. Of course, you will have to do the work to prevent fighting over these by making a schedule or finding a system that works for the class so that each child can be 100 percent certain that they will receive a fair turn. Scooters are particularly good for helping build and support core strength in children. You'd be surprised at how much of a nonissue they can become when you have a class properly balanced and working together harmoniously.

Advanced Ride and Read: (Start by Weeks 3–4)

This is the big payoff session, where your methodical hard work and their apparent chaos magically turn to gold. You've established rapport with your kids, you've just about mastered managing the class with your eyeballs, and most everyone is having a good time. Umberto isn't crying as much, Carl and Kendra have almost stopped fighting over the scooter, and Jadelyn is now more secure and comfortable with the routine of basic school. **The children trust you because they know you are going to let them physically move. Your class trusts you because they can depend on you that you will give them what they need.** They're excited and engaged because you've established that reading is an adventure of the imagination and absolutely achievable for everyone. This is where you formally begin your writing program. This is also the session where high reader Suzy, who has been rolling her eyes at how easy and immature this all is, gets her due.

Prepare Materials:

Gather a collection of wordless picture books and read one together each day. (At the end of this chapter, you can find a link to our ever-growing list of wordless picture books.) You will get through some quickly, while others will take three days!

> *Tip: Take your time during these read-alouds. This unit is designed to* **develop reading comprehension and critical thinking skills**. *It's essential you allow THEM to piece together the story, while asking probing questions to help push their thinking. Model your thinking out loud while reading wordless picture books: "I wonder why this turtle is looking so confused? Oh! That reminds me of a picture we saw before!" Allow children to do most of the thinking and talking while using the pictures to read. Don't be afraid to read favorites over again together. Your low decoders will be very satisfied with their ability to "read" a book, while your high decoders will be challenged to push their comprehension skills with more difficult wordless texts.*

Activity: After you've read a wordless book together as a group, take the wordless books you've collected and distribute one book at each chair. The children are now ready to practice their skills. Keep the same structure of "riding" and then stopping to "read." When they stop, they need to choose one place and stick with that one book. Keep them moving and wanting more by turning the light green and mixing it up again every two to five minutes or so, slowly increasing their 1:1 time with a book (your goal being to slowly extend the time they spend engaged in texts).

- ♦ Traffic signs are still around the room.
- ♦ Gradually extend the time of the reading and shorten the time of the riding.

Next steps and variations:

- ♦ Gradually add in new bins. As you add a bin, move from one book per chair to one bin of books at a table.
- ♦ Working out of table bins versus 1:1 books extends their reading time even further, so when the kids STOP

riding, they stay at the table they selected until they *ride again*. *Yeeha!*

- Aim to increase reading intervals at each table to 15 minutes; shorten as needed
- You can add in partner reading as an extension of the "find your partner" game or if you don't have enough books to go around. I usually save formal partner reading until January, but it's a nice way to extend the activity should you choose!

Progression of Book Collections:

- Wordless picture books
  - Wordless books provide a base of reading comprehension work and vary from the very simple to the extremely complex.
- Caldecott Award-winning picture books (introduce end of September)
  - Adding Caldecott books helps widen the spectrum of texts and helps readers and nonreaders tell more stories through reading pictures and words.
- Label books (introduce October)
  - Label books are books that have a picture and a word. These range in difficulty from board books to Richard Scarry-type books to field guides, architectural drawings, and books featuring diagrams.
- Author study (October–November)
  - An author study gives the opportunity for students to "become an expert" on an author's body of work, make text-to-text connections and observations, and engage in a project to share their knowledge and present their work to the community.

Year of Ride and Read: scaffolded reading and writing working together

The writing work each student produces in each unit is bound together. Collectively they form "chapters" of a year-long writing portfolio.

TABLE 2.1

Year of reading and writing working together

Month	*Reading*	*Writing*	*Word Work*	*Unit/Pacing*
September	Sign and Symbols *Nonfiction unit*	Physical movement, cut and paste	Sounds and symbols	Unit 1: Signs and Symbols Begin year with
Sept.–Oct.	Wordless Books	Drawing (blank paper, no lines)	Alphabet work, phonics	Start by week 3 or 4 of school
October	Caldecott Books	Drawing, partner share (blank paper, no lines)	Alphabet work, phonics	Add in by week 4 or 5 (Ends Unit 1)
Oct.–Nov.	Label books *Nonfiction unit*	Drawing and adding labels (blank paper, no lines)	Phonics work, matching word cards	Unit 2: Labels Start by weeks 4–6
November	First Project: Author Study	Draw, label, cut, and paste (blank paper, no lines)	Rhymes and Rhythms (work with your music teacher!)	Unit 3: Author Study Start by weeks 7–9
December	"How-To" Books *Nonfiction unit*	Sequencing with drawing and labeling (blank paper, or fold into fourths or sixths boxes or glue individual sequence squares onto larger paper	Sequence cards, phonics work, sight words	Unit 4: "How To" start by week 12 (unit ends with Winter break)
January	Character Study/ Author Study Launch formal reading program (small group structure, etc.)	Drawing, labeling, add speech bubbles, dialogue, onomatopoeia Blank paper, no lines. Can provide speech/thinking bubbles to cut out and add, or they can just draw them	Phonics work, sight words, digraphs Handwriting, fine motor work	Unit 5: Introducing New Routines and Character Study Returning from Winter/ Midyear break: three-week unit

February	Retelling Unit: Fairy Tales, graphic novels, comic strips "Stoplight Stories": Act out Plays	Draw, label, sequencing of story. Add speech bubbles to show dialogue between characters, fold paper in sixths and write in boxes – no lines	Sight words, connecting words	Unit 6: Fairy Tale Theater "Stoplight Stories" two to three weeks
March	Penny for a Poem: Perform Nursery Rhymes	Serves as the formal transition from blank paper to lined. Copy and print to help remember poem, draw and illustrate a nursery rhyme	Rhymes and Rhythms, transition to printing on lined paper; vowel work	Unit 6: "Penny for a Poem" one to two weeks
April	Nonfiction books Informational texts Biographies	Produce with a partner a book on a topic of their choosing including diagrams and labels (lined paper with space for diagrams and drawings) Each child produces a biography including: who, what, where, when, why, or how details (lined paper with space for drawing)	Writing full sentences, spacing between words, applying phonics, using resources around the room, sight words, long and short vowels	Unit 7: Non fiction Unit four- to six-week unit
May	Feelings Books	Full sentences with drawings (lined paper) They can add feeling after feeling – do "mad" one day, "happy" the next day, etc.	Writing full sentences, spacing between words, applying phonics, long and short vowels, using resources around the room; independently writing	Unit 8: Feelings Unit Wrap up year (can be as short as a week or as long as three weeks, as needed)

Scaffolded Writing Program

Start to slowly fold in your writing program. Keep it simple. Children are happy and feel successful starting with drawing. Don't rush past this key representational stage. Let them draw and verbally share their stories.

- Have the children draw their own story and "read" it to a partner. Pictures tell stories!
- You can expand on this by having them record their storytelling or by making short videos documenting their work.
- Be sure to incorporate cut and paste into your writing time in September and October. Observing their approach to a cut and paste project is one of the best assessment tools available to you.
- Use this time to assess hand grip, alphabet knowledge, phonics, social interactions, and to record observational data.
- Encourage kids to label their drawings starting with your label unit, introduce label books, and work on having students apply phonics to create labels for their drawings.

Paper for Writing and Putting It All Together

You can use any size of paper for writing. What's important is that you start with blank paper and WAIT to transition to lined paper until spring. This may sound late in the year, but delaying adding in the challenge of formal writing on a line gives children a longer time to focus on the *application of phonics* without juggling printing and creating formal sentences, which adds a significant degree of difficulty. Waiting longer to make the transition to lined paper and formal sentences also honors a child's time line of development by allowing for a wider breadth and time to do a lot of prework and skill development essential to "putting it all together." By the time you transition to lined paper, they already see themselves as writers and the transition is barely noticed. Try it and you will see a tremendous difference in their confidence, excitement, and ability as writers.

Suggested scaffolding of writing paper:

- September–January: 11 × 17, blank
- Fold into sixths for December "How-To" unit and February story boxes
- March: 11 × 17, add lines with space for drawing (focus on copying text to lined paper)
- April: putting it all together – nonfiction project includes topic web, drawings, labels, and writing sentences on lines to create a book with a partner
- May–June: lined paper with space for drawings; create an individual "Feelings Book"

First Project: November Author Study

Congratulations! Getting through the first eight weeks and Halloween is a huge accomplishment! Time to celebrate by mixing up the routine and starting a nice big project.

The work of Eric Carle is an excellent choice for many reasons. His books are numerous, engaging, beautiful, and vary in reading difficulty levels, so you can easily target both your high and low readers with engaging texts. Many of his books also use and build on repetition and pattern, which helps your nonreaders "read" through recognizing patterns and picture-word association. Also, many of his books are easy to read using musical rhythms: a regular beat, call and response, or chant to help your class build early reading skills. Whichever author you choose to study here, make sure their work contains a wide range of difficulty of reading levels, solid picture-word associations, and the ability to create chants, rhymes, and rhythms while reading some of the texts.

Finding the Beat and Using Picture Cues

Use books that help readers use a beat to start to track words with their fingers and give them the ability to tell the story through pictures. Use books that can be easily adapted into little plays for your class to act out as well as made into appealing chants to help prove to pre-readers that they really are readers!

Books Become "Plays to Perform"

Practice translating books into short performances and reading and practicing them each day until you get a few of these performances down to showcase as part of your final project celebration. Use rhythm sticks, shakers, and clapping to help students stay on the beat of the book. Work with your music teacher to help you!

Discovering Text-to-Text Connections; Matching Picture and Words

Help your class "discover" similarities together when reading together by letting them make observations and connections between one author's texts. Model your thinking: "hmm, this book reminds me of another one." It should all be their own idea! Some classes will make more connections than others but resist the temptation to do the thinking for them. Make them do the heavy lifting. This is also a nice place to start partner reading.

Introducing More Difficult Texts

Introduce more difficult texts and continue to think out loud while reading to model the work of reading comprehension, of using picture cues to help find and point to words, and look for connections between texts. These books might be too hard for most kids in your class to read, but they now have skills they can draw on to help them dig deeper into a book and enjoy it on a new level.

Presenting Their Work at the Museum and Café

There are three parts to this final project, each showcasing a different piece of the puzzle of early reading skills. You can start with one part so it's not overwhelming and as you build skills year after year, add the next piece.

1. Theater: *(chant, rhythm, music, and movement)* The easiest place to start is by performing several of the little chant plays to an audience. Add a few hats or simple costumes and props and, voila! You've got a show! The kids feel

accomplished and kindergarten has something to share with the community by November! Invite parents!

2. Illustration showcase: *(fine motor, perception, spatial thinking, organization and planning, teamwork, color study, writing, speaking)* Have a theater show and then head over to "open" the museum where children can show their drawings, collages, and illustrations related to the author study. Students can have created a plan for their illustration, drawing, and labeling of all the words, pieces, and colors they want to use in their work as well as an actual piece they've created, inspired by the author's work.

   Finish up with a lesson on biographies, write theirs up, and display it alongside their finished works in a "museum" along with their book. Kids stand in front of their work to tell visitors about the process of making the piece. Invite your school community to come! The finished illustration makes a nice end-of-the-school year or holiday gift to families.
3. How to create the Café: (*a bonanza of movement, self-regulation, and executive functioning*) This is by far the trickiest to pull off, but it's also one of the most effective activities for working on and showcasing self-regulation. By the end of this complex activity, you will know who struggles and who excels in the area of executive functioning. You can do this with half of your class "working" at the Museum greeting visitors while the other half works the Café, and then switch groups.

Step 1: Server Trainings

You can fold this "training" in at any point in the project, but beware, it catches on like wildfire and they will all want a turn. If you can get some little aprons, it definitely ups the ante to get "certified" in "server training." Basically the kids are practicing balancing, focus, and concentration, but it makes it more exciting to be in "server training." Invent achievable, scaffolded levels to build up the imagined, playful, intensity, and importance.

Level 1: Put one or two empty paper cups balanced on a tray – take three laps around the classroom (make up a route)
Level 2: Add water to the cups (they do a set number of laps)
Level 3: Add more cups, water – maximum of three (do laps)
Level 4: If you want to use real teacups, (espresso cups are perfect), add in those – keep in mind, then you'll also have to train a dishwasher too (a highly popular job!)
Level 5: Put (imaginary or real) food on a plate (laps)
Level 6: Three cups with water and food (laps)
Level 7: Chef training: chef pours water into the cups; helps trains new trainees
Level 8: Cashier and hostess training (math integration)
Level 9: Manager: Trainer of all jobs

Vary as needed. You can make the routes more challenging as well. You might be surprised at who is challenged or excited by this task!

IMAGE 2.1
Tray with coffee and cookie for café serving

Step 2: Math Integration

Build in some work with coins and money so your class is prepared to handle nickels and dimes. Servers work with money all the time!

Step 3: Play and Practice

Set up a "restaurant" and play pretend where some kids are customers and some kids are servers. Do this for at least a week before you launch your actual café so they can get a system down. Teachers and kids work together as an authentic team to come up with systems to make the Café run more smoothly.

Step 4: Bring It to Life

Either bake, buy, or have parents send in food and drink donations for the day of your café. It doesn't matter if you are serving free hot water and dry crackers for a dime. The kids will be excited to be "real workers" responsible for doing a job. You can see them physically grow during this process, at least in confidence as they realize, "I can do this!" Parents and members of your school community can come in for the theater performance, to view their child's work in the Museum and to be seated and served in the Café. Set the scene with a little music and you're in business! It can be a bit unwieldy at first, but with practice, you'll get better at managing it all!

Moving Forward

This sequence of structured skills and projects is designed to improve young children's literacy skills through movement, attention, observation, immersion, participation, self-regulation and executive functioning skill work, and awareness of shape, line, sound, rhythm, and reading comprehension. Add in your own phonics, word work, and additional literacy centers as time allows, as indicated in our "Year-At-A-Glance" downloadable supplement available to you.

It is our hope that the "Ride and Read" approach and structure to teaching reading and writing expands the scope of how literacy is often taught to young children, especially as definitions of literacy are rapidly expanding to include a world increasingly communicating through codes, symbols, pictures, video, expression, and multitudes of languages.

Math: Inquiry, Centers, Skills, and Teamwork

Establishing Inquiry and the Math Mind

Teachers of young children are often shy around mathematics and in some cases, avoid teaching it as much as possible. You as a practitioner must make your peace with math if you haven't already. It's OK if you flunked algebra two and can't remember how to multiply fractions because you haven't done it since the fourth grade. Recognize that mathematics is often taught as a memorization of a sequence of skills that go largely unused once you leave high school. It's not your fault that you can't remember the Pythagorean theorem. You were "taught" it, you memorized it, passed or flunked the test, and promptly forgot it. Recognize that memorizing procedures without context or understanding is exactly why you can't remember. Ask yourself what that type of teaching and learning accomplishes.

Even if you were successful in math and can do a computational full twisting algorithm, start by asking yourself and really thinking deeply about, "what is math?" In the world of standards and academia, math is numbers and operations, geometry, data, and measurement. Work to make yourself find real examples of each of these concepts in daily life. Ask yourself what the point of it all is; ask yourself that question over and over again as a continuous mental exercise.

Math is patterns, logic, truth, mental agility, beauty, creativity, symbols, systems, space, time, construction, architecture, art, science, code building and deciphering, data, graphing, abstract representations, collections of objects, nature, analysis, statistics, and equality. That all sounds far more intriguing than how we've been systematically downsized to think about mathematics, doesn't it? Space and time?! Yes, please! Find wonder in it! The pursuit and appreciation of the mathematical world is key ongoing practice for you as a professional. You cannot teach what you don't have an appreciation for!

Mathematics is some of the most elegant, creative, fun, and logical thinking we as humans can do. Sit with that statement for a bit. Where can YOU as a teacher see that playing out? Spend some time thinking and stretching your mind to free it from the constructs you were taught. For example, when learning to "carry and borrow" in subtraction, you were taught to follow a "recipe" of how to do the process versus actually taught to think about what you were doing when subtracting. When you "learned" the procedure, you were told that you couldn't take 5 away from 3 in 53-15 so you had to go borrow from the 10s place. However, that's incorrect. You CAN absolutely take 5 from 3, it's -2. So 50-10 = 40-2 = 38. We don't credit children with the ability to handle negative numbers, though, instead teaching recipes designed to get them to perform a series of math skills.

Areas of focus for math in early education:

1. Inquiry: questioning, documenting, using logic, and providing evidence
2. Applications: real-world centers for play, exploration, research, and trials
3. Skill support centers
4. Teamwork Tables

Inquiry, Documenting, Using Logic and Providing Evidence

Making a list of everything your students know and perceive about "what is math" is your first step to creating a dynamic mathematical community of inquiry. Kids have a broad conception of math terms: money, shapes, adding, multiplication aka "times," clocks, numbers, measuring. Developing mathematical inquiry takes time and your constant attention in terms of helping children wonder, question, and record their findings. Work to shape your class in this ongoing practice through daily mathematical whole-class conversations.

1. Inquiry -----> refine through exploration -----> public questions -----> logic and error detection -----> practice trials -----> proof and consensus

2. The math neighborhood: mathematical exploration and application

3. Exploration -----> materials help self-correct -----> practice -----> application -----> documentation -----> share out -----> next question

Any type of skill development requires a "hook" – a rationale, an application, motivation, a need; form follows function. This is the component missing from so many of the programs we've seen out there. While there are always a few kids who are genuinely motivated and interested, most kids really DO NOT CARE 2 + 3 = 5 and 3 + 2 = 5 and 5-3 = 2. In their minds they think, "OK, that's nice, lady." If you are lucky and they like you, they will humor you while you give a picture-perfect lesson, but what they all really want to know is, "when can we play again?!"

We aren't saying direct instruction, quality lessons, and instructions don't matter, or that kids aren't motivated to learn. We ARE saying that play is 100 percent where children's heads and hearts are – never forget that! And play is not a frivolous thing. It's essential you recognize their need for it, honor it, and USE IT as a teaching tool they will naturally understand and gravitate toward.

Applications: Real-World Centers for Play, Exploration, Research, and Trials

In the home, crafts, construction, cooking, and family game time is where math is most visible. Children can see math in the larger world as well: grocery stores, restaurants, banks, gyms. Take advantage of your town or neighborhood as sources of math and make sure children have experience with these everyday places by bringing them to your classroom play centers as part of your math curriculum. While Josie plays with and handles coins and money working at "Brownie's Bank," Marcus is doing five sets of ten reps with weights in "Workout World" and Jose follows 1-2-3 footwork position directions in your makeshift dance studio. Oh yes, it's math! Glorious, moving, playing, relevant math they will adore. Who knew math was SO MUCH FUN?

Sample play centers:

- ◆ Bank
- ◆ Grocery store
- ◆ Restaurant
- ◆ Construction zones
- ◆ Workout World
- ◆ Music center
- ◆ Dance studio

We discuss at length how to set up your classroom space to help you maximize these "play math" neighborhood centers. The trick to these centers is finding a balance between play and skill development. Your timing matters here: introduce too much structure and the center bombs; not enough and it can fizzle. If no one is interested after a few days, try again another time. The best thing to do is to keep your ear open to what they are already playing and be ready with your pop-up center materials. Keep centers very basic to begin with; listen and observe your class working and playing; and feed their needs by supplying structure through manipulatives, menus, money, bank accounts, time cards, receipts, and 1-2-3 step directions.

Skill Support Centers

Skill development in math can get tricky – too much and you start narrowing the curriculum and focusing too much on the "achievement" of metrics; too little and you risk some children missing important skills. Note we said some: whether it be math, reading, or social-emotional skills, it is clear that some children need more support and guidance than others. Part of your job is to begin to identify these children, discover where they need assistance, and build in support. Classroom observations, interviews, questions, and documentation help you identify children who need support and in what area.

Skill supports should follow rather than lead. Leading with skills results in half your class eventually "being bored" as they've already "mastered" the concept and creating a culture of covering skills. Too often, math is viewed as a coverage of skills you either "get" or you don't and then are either remedialized or passed on in order to achieve the next set of skills.

Children need and enjoy experience doing workbook activities, playing games, and working with manipulatives. Direct instruction and practice with specific skill work should be targeted and informed by the data you collect through observations, writing samples, and conversations.

Teamwork Tables

Young children want to play with math and manipulatives. Manipulatives help bring forth abstract mathematical skills and concepts to visible creations and representations, and are central to any program. Young children need LOTS of time to explore math tools and will always use them in interesting ways. It's tempting to say children will use them the "wrong" way, as they will spend months happily building towers with cuisenaire rods, but let them. It's important children have the opportunity to fully explore the materials so they are ready for the concept when it comes. As with anything, timing is everything and especially so with children on a developmental continuum. Devote the entire first three months of math time toward the children working with various math manipulatives; working at Teamwork Tables to construct, build, discover, and manipulate. Slowly add in more structure to these centers as the kids are ready for it. Again, your observations are critical in knowing when to strike with the right question or new material to help guide their inquiry.

Your class will likely spend a large part of the year making "the longest train EVER" with Unifix cubes. Coordinating them by pattern and color comes later developmentally. At first, they just want to make the train REALLY LONG. How long can we make it?! How can we know? Celebrate the teamwork, exuberance, and joy that goes into the project.

Math Is . . .

- cooperative.
- teamwork.
- fun.

- important and all around us.
- uses props, toys, and manipulatives to help show your thinking.
- number work, shapes, money, adding and taking away.
- something that "makes sense."
- truth.
- drawing, writing, recording, labeling, secret shortcuts, and codes.

When teams are ready, introduce problems for them to solve. They can work together to figure out which tools will help them solve the problem and best show their thinking. Your ultimate aim is for teams to be able to work together to construct, question, discuss, and share their thinking with one another while working together to solve math problems.

A team approach is important for several reasons: it helps develop mathematical conversations, vocabulary, and thinking. Teams help develop social skills around taking turns, leadership, and learning to be both wrong and right gracefully. Approaching mathematics through teams that are not competitive, but rather cooperative in the goal of arriving at the truth, helps formulate positive associations with math and creates a culture, with students sharing their thinking and working to reach consensus. Keep teams fresh by rotating them every month and strategically mixing up the groupings to help shape thinking and skill development.

Games

Note on games: ninety-nine percent of math games for young children are too complicated, often resulting in frustration, confusion, and fatigue. Simplify games to help target the skill sets you are trying to focus on: subitizing, moving fluently on a number line, doing addition and subtraction, and taking turns. All you need is a number line, dice, and a couple of characters for the kids to move. To them, moving a *toy human* figurine along a number line is a COMPLETELY DIFFERENT GAME than moving a little *toy animal* figurine along the exact same number line. They'll eventually figure out that it's actually the same game, but it's OK to let that play out!

Supporting Scientific Inquiry

Science is a favorite among little kids. They see scientists in cartoons and stories: the "mad scientist" or the potion-making wizard or witch. Young children are eager to play at science, create, imagine, and learn. It's sad that early science is often reduced to "Guess how many seeds are in this apple or pumpkin and record your answers in this apple packet." After that "unit" every fall, the entire subject is often left alone and forgotten for the rest of the year.

Year-Long Inquiry

With the inquiry approach, science forms the basis of your entire curriculum through a year-long study on trees. Why trees? Because a child can see them and they are large and impressive. Because we need them to sustain human, animal, and insect life. Trees vary by geography and are "readable" by their leaves and characteristics. We depend on trees for paper,

IMAGE 2.2
"Where we see wood" thought web

wood, food, and air. Trees are vacuum cleaners for pollution and hold hands in networks under the earth to prevent erosion. Additionally, trees make a good inquiry unit because humans have come to be more capable of identifying advertising symbols than the nature around us. Just google "apple" and see the top hit. It's no longer a tree but a product. Which can YOU identify by sight?

Mini-units

Throughout the year, insert mini-units throughout your curriculum. Create mini kits designed to promote projects and lines of inquiry such as

- outside play: walks, discoveries, and tools for exploration.
- inventions and "Things That Go": pulleys, wheels, ropes, levers, and inclined planes.
- codes and computing.
- ongoing bird study as part of tree inquiry.
- Weekly Lab Kits:
  - rocks
  - magnets
  - Sink and Float
  - potions
  - stars, sun, moon, and planets
- Woody's Woodshop: constructions: nuts and bolts, hammers, nails, materials for cutting and attaching

Save indoor units for bad weather days and winter, and work outside as much as you can the rest of the time. (This will also help you tuck in some extra play if you are in a setting that doesn't value play.) SCIENCE!

Show What You Know

As you observe these mini-units in action, be sure to listen, observe, and write down the thinking process of the group. Reflect those conversations in group discussions and openly discuss: "I see you are thinking differently now. Can you share what changed your mind?" and more back-and-forth discussion around the topic. Formulating good questions is quite a talent and takes years to perfect.

Woven throughout the literacy curriculum are nonfiction texts, culminating with the "Nonfiction STEM fair," where students choose topics to explore. They read nonfiction books and work to develop their own lines of inquiry. At the end of the project, students present their work.

Sample student checklist for STEM nonfiction center showcase

Your STEM nonfiction centers must contain the following elements:

- Three reference books
- Activities for a little kid to do to learn about your center
- A book written by you and your partner on your subject
- A math component
- A tech element
- An invention or original design

End-of-Year Celebration of Year-Long Tree Study

Celebrate your year-long inquiry by showcasing all of the work you've collectively and individually done surrounding trees. Share your class dialogues, findings, photographs, and constructions. Have the children lead their caregiver on a walk, pointing out the trees around them and following a map of their own creation. Create a documentary throughout the year and share it; have children make their own books or a class book. Have a "Tree Fair" featuring all the products we use from trees. However you choose to celebrate the end of your year-long study, be sure to showcase your students' process of wonderings, recording of data and information, drawings, creations, and ultimately, knowledge.

Social Studies: Keeping Community

Before we dive into specific units, it's important for you as a professional to stay current, informed, and curious about all academic and cultural topics, but especially as related to diversity, equity, and inclusion as your students come to you from many different cultural backgrounds, identities, and life experiences.

- It is essential that you as a professional work to represent multiple perspectives of history equitably, and that you work to unlearn history from a white colonization perspective. Do not teach stereotypes or misinformation.
- Teachers should be able to model open, engaging, and equitable dialogue about any topic a child might be curious about.
- Ensure you have multiple skin tone crayons and papers available, and have open and frequent conversations about the diversity of humans.
- Ensure your classroom represents diverse populations throughout your class library, artwork, displays, dolls, toys, and larger curriculum.
- Continuously work to update, refine, and hone your curriculum to be within the guidelines of the "Learning for Justice" Frameworks for K–2.

Social studies is an abstract concept for most young children, so begin by using your classroom environment to set the stage. Following are a few key units of study and conversational topics to explore with young children:

"All about Me" Identity unit

- Humans come in all shapes, sizes, ages, and colors.
- Each child has value, importance, and is likable and loved just the way they are.
- Families are all different.
- Grown-ups should help kids, never hurt them.

- Everyone is good at some things and struggles with some things.
- Every student has work displayed showing a representation of themselves and some things they like or enjoy.

Community Unit

- Your classroom is a community.
- Communities work together and help one another.
- Kids clean and care for the classroom.
- There are roles and responsibilities essential to every community.

"People in Our Neighborhood"

Explore your school community! Take a walk through your school as if it were a friendly neighborhood. Make a map of your classroom and then of your school. Greet people by name and ask them a little about themselves. Your class should know by name:

- anyone who helps with drop-off or dismissal.
- anyone who serves food.
- anyone who helps clean the school.
- school administrators.
- school administrative assistants and clerical staff.
- the nurse and/or any support staff they might come in contact with.
- their bus driver if they take the bus.
- the name of the town mayor.

"Fair and Unfair" Rules (Ongoing throughout the Year)

- Leaders can make fair or unfair rules.
- Why might a leader make unfair rules?
- What can you do when a leader makes an unfair rule?
- What do places/schools/towns/countries do when there are unfair rules?
- What kind of leader do you want to be?
- Peacemakers play an important role in the classroom and in the world.

- Peacemakers stand up against injustice by using words, through writing, and through peaceful actions or protests.

"Back Then": Sequencing and Discovering History

- There are things that happened "Back Then." See what the kids mention and know, print out pictures, and have them think about what came first, next, last.
- History is full of stories – it's saying "Hi" to real stories from the past.
- Sometimes people get so embarrassed about the bad things they did to hurt people, they worked to "cover up" the story. "Hi-stories" are always being uncovered and that's what's so fun and interesting about it!

Importance of the Arts

Art always seems like the first thing to be taken away from traditional school models, but it should absolutely be among the last. Art brings together every facet of a curriculum, breathing color, imagination, form, structure, magic, and life into any topic worthy of study or inquiry.

Too often art is reduced to "creativity": "here, go in this room and 'get creative' for forty-five minutes," as if it's a light switch to be turned on at assigned times. While art as a pursuit may have degrees of creativity to it, so does mathematics – often spectacularly so. Art should be thought of as possessing the same rigor and intensity as any subject and be treated as having the same core value and importance as math or reading. An art program is essential to a quality education and should be fully integrated throughout core subjects.

Children's artwork is an expression of their learning. Children naturally gravitate toward drawing and it is their first form of written communication. We as educators should recognize children's drawings as expressions as worthy and as valuable as any high school essay. Children's artistic creations are expressions of their learning.

There is a vast space between artwork and a craft project. Precut fruit glued onto a paper cornucopia or cotton balls placed on a sheep is not artwork. Googly eyes on a pumpkin does not inspire wonder or reflect any learning. While crafts may have some value in terms of following 1-2-3 step directions, that is construction, not artwork. A good art project means you can tell "whose is whose" without any names on them or the complete opposite – when it doesn't matter who did what and it's a collaborative expression worked on by the entire community.

As a professional, keep pushing yourself to learn more about art. Study the work of Joan Miro, Cy Twombly, Jean-Michel Basquiat, and think about how it relates to the process of children's writing. Think about the words of Pablo Picasso, "It took me four years to paint like Raphael but a lifetime to paint like a child."

Assessment Checklist: Things Every Kindergartner Should Do

Every day:

- Read (or be read to)
- Write
- Draw
- Count
- Sing
- Dance
- Create or build
- Play outside
- Play inside
- Rest

Every week:

- Explore new materials, media, and sensory experiences
- Write or draw in a journal or logbook
- Go outdoors (preferably beyond school grounds) to explore the world and experience changes in weather (this in addition to regular recess)

Every month:

- Learn about a new author, illustrator, or type of book
- Cook/bake/prepare and taste a shared meal or snack
- Learn at least two new songs, rhymes, poems, or finger plays

Over the course of a year:

- Observe and document the life cycle of two different living things
- Try at least one new physical activity or sport
- Learn about the life and work of three different artists or illustrators
- Enjoy at least one live or recorded theater, music, or dance performance
- Celebrate at least three cultural holidays from around the world
- Perform in front of an audience
- Participate in an age-appropriate (collective or individual) research project
- Write and send a card or letter through the mail
- Perform an act of kindness or charity to support someone less fortunate
- Visit and explore at least one natural area, either in person or virtually
- Plan, create, and present a gift for a family member or other loved one.
- Compare and contrast different versions of a familiar story or fable
- Make a friend in another grade or classroom
- Discover and share at least three things that make him or her unique and special
- Formally express gratitude and appreciation for someone who has helped him or her

References and Recommended Reading

Carle, E. (2010). *The Very Collection Hardcover Complete Set: Busy Spider, Clumsy Click Beetle, Hungry Caterpillar, Lonely Firefly, Quiet Cricket.* Penguin Young Readers Group.

Chiarello, E. (2012). *Social justice: The Teaching Tolerance Anti-Bias Standards.* [PDF File]. www.tolerance.org/sites/default/files/2017-06/TT_Social_Justice_Standards_0.pdf

Echternacht, H., & Murray, A. (eds). (n.d.) *Kinderchat wordless picture book bin.* https://docs.google.com/document/d/1GCeYeZ5Ac2exRnUMGMBDhhDy_3egi7X2VsW8ojsEPLs/edit#

Hoban, T. (1987). *I read signs.* Greenwillow Books.

Scarry, R. (1963). *The best word book ever.* Golden Press.

3

Yellow: Child Development

As we have been known to say at #kinderchat: we don't teach programs, we teach CHILDREN. That said: most experienced teachers report that their teacher preparation program did not equip them with a strong foundation in what it actually means to be surrounded by five-year-olds all day, every day. Why do they tell such bad jokes? Why are some of them SO BOSSY? Why do they melt into tearful puddles at pick-up time, even if they have had a great day? Why do they wiggle SO MUCH? What is with the constant wrestling? Understanding these things not only helps you teach these tiny, complicated creatures; it will help you stay sane while doing so!

The Basics of Child Development and Why It Matters

The Core of It All: Essential Ongoing Study

In kindergarten, perhaps more than any other level, we teach CHILDREN first, not a curriculum or subject area. Understanding children, studying children, coming back over and over to resources about child development all form the foundation of what we do. When you are stuck on a problem, whether it is academic or behavioral, go back to learning about *children*. When a child is doing something is annoying you, understand WHY they do it. Deepen your knowledge of children, their needs, development, tendencies. Your job is the ongoing understanding of children.

To do this well, you will need to be intentional about this. One of the best ways is to look for professional development (PD) opportunities that will help you know more about kids. Most teacher preparation programs do not do a good job of teaching about children; they focus on instruction and curriculum but not on **children**. At best, in most programs, you get one very basic developmental psych class. This is not a sturdy enough foundation to spend seven hours a day surrounded by five-year-olds.

One of the easiest ways to expand your knowledge base is to look for PD opportunities from other fields. Conferences, workshops, webinars, and books from the fields of psychology, occupational therapy, therapy/counseling, social work, recreation, neuroscience, and childcare can all be valuable to teachers, too.

Having a strong child development lens will help you assess materials, curricula, resources, and technology for use in your classroom. Being grounded in child development makes you a better, more informed advocate for your students and yourself.

Staying True to Developmentally Appropriate Practice (DAP)

What Is DAP?

This is a term that gets thrown around a lot, but what does it actually mean? While you can google a million, perfectly acceptable definitions, at its core, and for our purposes here, **DAP means that *the expectations, routines, and experiences that occur in your classroom are appropriate to the age and developmental level of your students.*** You cannot expect five-year-olds to be able to do the same things as 12-year-olds or eight-year-olds, or even six-year-olds. To teach five-year-olds, we must honor their five-year-old-ness.

Simultaneously, DAP also means that **all** areas of children's growth and development are honored, fostered, and supported in your classroom. These areas include:

- social-emotional development
- cognitive and intellectual development
- physical development

To do all of this well, we first need a good working knowledge of five-year-olds. We will provide an overview here, but we also strongly recommend that every teacher of young children keep the following books at their fingertips:

- A good child development textbook, published within the last ten years. We like Laura Berk's work, but the textbook for any introductory undergraduate course in early childhood education or developmental psychology will probably serve you well, as long as it covers birth to age eight. Brand-new textbooks are expensive; check your local university or community college for used editions, or go for a cheaper e-book version. Ideally, read the whole book. Child development is SUPER interesting and fairly miraculous! If the whole book is too daunting, read three chapters: the chapter that covers five-year-olds, and the chapters before/after. (You will need to know a little bit about three- and four-year-olds, and a little bit about six- to eight-year-olds. We'll talk about this in a minute.)
- The most recent version of the National Association for the Education of Young Children's (NAEYC's) *Developmentally Appropriate Practice in Early Childhood Programs*. This is a guide to implementing DAP in your classroom, and it includes specific examples of what DAP looks like (and does not look like) in a kindergarten setting. As of this writing, the most recent version was from 2009, with a new edition forthcoming.

Development versus Learning

You may have noticed that our emphasis in this chapter so far has been on children's development, and not on their learning. But isn't learning what matters most when we are talking about school? The short answer is that yes, of course, learning is the focus of any classroom; however, learning cannot happen effectively if it does not align with children's development. Learned skills rely on developmental processes, and if the development has not occurred, the skill cannot be learned.

- A **developmental process** refers to a sequence of development that occurs in a predictable order, within a consistent time frame, for all typically developing children. Learning to walk and talk are examples of developmental processes.
- A **learned skill** is exactly what it says: a skill that can be learned, and that relies on opportunity, exposure, practice, and sometimes instruction for a child (or anyone) to master it. Depending on culture, geography, values, opportunity, and resources, not all children will develop the same set of learned skills.

Riding a bike is a learned skill that relies on developmental processes. To learn to ride a bike, a child must have completed a number of developmental processes that start in infancy: holding their head up, sitting upright, standing upright, maintaining and adjusting balance, focusing their eyes at various distances, coordinating their eyes and body to reach a particular destination, and so on. Until a child can do all of these things, they will not be able to successfully ride a bicycle. At the same time, even when a child has reached all the appropriate stages of development, they will not learn to ride a bike unless they have access to a bicycle, time and opportunity to practice, and perhaps some instruction.

The relationship between development and learning is foundational to teaching kindergarten. If a child is struggling with a particular learning outcome, it may be because they have not yet completed the necessary developmental processes. A toddler who cannot yet ride a bike does not need more time on the bike, or more instruction on HOW to ride a bike. They need time for their body proportions to mature, which will move their center of gravity, which will improve their overall balance ... The same may be true of a five-year-old who cannot yet copy a sentence from the board into their journal.

All About Five-Year-Olds

Introductory note: We know that the entry age for kindergarten varies regionally, and that depending on where you are, your kindergarten students may be anywhere from four to six years old when the school year begins. We are focusing on five-year-olds as a baseline. The textbook we mentioned in the previous section will help you scale up or down, depending on your students' ages.

The points highlighted below are things that are most likely to be visible and relevant in a classroom setting; this is by no means an exhaustive list of everything that five-year-olds can or can't yet do!

Language Development

Between the ages of five and six, most typically developing children:

- speak in complex sentences.
- can be easily understood when speaking.
- retell the plots of familiar stories or movies with good accuracy.
- use pronouns correctly (he/she/they/we).
- use past tenses accurately, with some overgeneralization for irregular verbs ("I swimmed across the pool.").
- use future tense appropriately ("I will go home after school.").

Physical Development

Between the ages of five and six, most typically developing children:

- will begin losing teeth.
- can walk backward.
- can skip and run forward efficiently.
- can go up and down stairs with alternating feet.
- have developed a preference for one hand.
- may not yet be able to consistently cross the midline of their own body (that is, placing their right hand on their left ear or knee).
- can "pump" (or learn to pump) on a swing.
- can jump down from surfaces up to half their own height.
- may struggle to jump up onto a curb from two feet, or to jump over a line/stick/and so on.
- can comfortably climb ladders, monkey bars, and so on, and are quite fearless about doing so.
- pick up small objects using a pincer grasp (thumb and one or two fingers).
- can use a spoon and a fork effectively.
- cannot yet use a knife to cut their own food.
- go from being energetic to exhausted very quickly.
- seek sensory input, especially through touch and movement.

Social and Emotional Development

Between the ages of five and six, most typically developing children:

- seek out and enjoy interactions with peers.
- develop "best" or strongly preferred friends.
- can separate calmly from a parent to go with a known adult, and may do so with new adults, as well.
- enjoy and seek out interaction with known, nonparental adults.
- Seek approval from authority figures.

- have and can express favorites/preferences: colors, foods, clothing.
- enjoy cooperative dramatic play with peers, acting out complex storylines.
- continue to be attached to comfort objects such as stuffed animals or blankets.
- are beginning to be able to willfully control their own emotions: sometimes attempting not to cry when they are hurt or upset; trying not to laugh during circle time; and so on.

Cognitive and Intellectual Development

Between the ages of five and six, most typically developing children:

- enjoy sorting and classifying objects and people (this can lead to a strong focus on "boy" versus "girl" things/colors/behaviors).
- make comparisons based on size, shape, color, and characteristics.
- place importance on being older/bigger/first.
- can remain attentive and independently engaged in an enjoyable activity for at least five full minutes.
- can count at least five objects accurately.
- understand rules and enjoy enforcing them.
- begin to enjoy competitive games and to value winning.
- know what is real and what is imaginary or made-up.
- know how to lie, and can do so to their own advantage (to get out of "trouble" or to get the outcome they want).
- enjoy jokes and may enjoy making others laugh.
- can predict familiar events based on contextual clues (If we are eating a snack, recess is next.).
- have a beginning sense of narrative structure (the beginning, middle, end of a story).
- are able to describe the chronology of a short series of events, and to say if one event happened before or after another.

- have a very inaccurate sense of the passage of time: something that happened "a long time ago" may have been this morning, while something that occurred "yesterday" may actually have been last week or last month.

Self-Care

By the time they start kindergarten, most typically developing children are able (or able to learn to):

- use the toilet entirely independently, including wiping.
- put on their own outerwear: coat, boots or shoes, hat, mittens, snow gear.
- use a fork and spoon efficiently.
- recognize their own belongings.

They often are not able to:

- tie their shoes.
- use a knife to cut their food.
- open a milk carton or juice box.
- start the zipper on their coat.
- reliably put their shoes on the correct feet.
- read.

> *A word on red-shirting*
>
> *Red-shirting is the term used to describe the relatively recent phenomenon of (mostly upper- and middle-class) parents choosing to hold their child back a year before the child starts kindergarten, when the child has a birthday that is very close to the age cutoff for their district. For example, in a district where children must turn five before October 1 of their kindergarten year, parents of children with September birthdays may choose to wait an extra year before the child begins school. In our view, this practice is most common in districts where the kindergarten program is not developmentally appropriate for the ages of the children who are enrolling. If a kindergarten program is appropriate for the ages of the children who attend, there is no reason to delay attendance.*

Five Things Five-Year-Olds Do and the Developmental Reasons Why They Do Them:

- Tattling: They like rules and enforcing them; they like interacting and seeking approval from authority figures; they like categorizing things/people as good or bad.
- Wiggling and fidgeting: They can sustain attention for short periods of time; they will seek sensory input to remain alert and engaged.
- Wrestling/playing rough: They are exploring risk; they value being bigger and stronger; they are seeking peer interaction and sensory input; they are exploring cause and effect and physical strength.
- Playing elaborate games of pretend: they are exploring the difference between real and imaginary; they are building narratives; they are exploring the chronology of events.
- Bossing each other around: they are exploring authority; they are seeking the approval of authority figures; they like rules.

Schemas: Wisdom from the United Kingdom

One of the many things we have learned through years of talking with exceptional teachers from the United Kingdom has been the concept of *schemas*. Schemas are defined as "repeated actions and behaviors to find out how things work." This definition also helps explain why young children are quite happy to engage in the same types of play over and over. A few common examples are:

- Enclosing: children putting things in enclosed spaces – including themselves!
- Trajectory: children throwing things and being fascinated with moving things
- Enveloping: wrapping things; building forts
- Positioning: lining things up
- Connecting: connecting things together with tape, glue; sewing
- Rotational: wheels, spinning

- Transforming: mixing, cooking, mud
- Transporting: moving objects from one place to another

Teachers in England document and make note of when children are engaged in this type of developmental work. At the end of this chapter, you can find a link to a guide created by teacher Kathie Brodie; this guide describes each schema, explains what is being explored and learned within each one, and suggests materials to support this schema in your classroom. If you have spent any time at all with young children, you can certainly picture a real-life example for most of them!

Executive Functioning and Self-Regulation

Executive Functioning

The term "executive functioning" is thrown around with increasing frequency in discussions around education. It refers to the brain functions that allow us to plan, initiate, and complete tasks. The Harvard Center on the Developing Child identifies three primary components of executive functioning:

1. Working memory: the ability to hold information in your head and apply it to your current task or context
2. Self-control: the ability to manage impulses and follow a plan
3. Mental flexibility: the ability to direct our attention appropriately, and to shift our focus when needed

Kids with weak executive function may:

- struggle to organize and plan tasks.
- leave a trail of belongings behind them.
- be unable to choose and manage the materials necessary for an activity.
- skip steps when completing a task.
- struggle to persist with a task all the way to completion, even when the task is appropriate to their skill level.

You can see how these abilities (or lack thereof) can become crucial in a classroom setting. The good news for us as educators is that executive functioning skills can be explicitly taught, modeled, and reinforced in a classroom, using some of the games, routines, and practices that we share later in this chapter.

Self-Regulation

Self-regulation is the visible and functional manifestation of a child (or adult's) executive functioning skills. It has also become a bit of a buzzword in the world of education, and while there is good reason for this, this popularity has also obscured the true meaning of the term. It has often been oversimplified and interpreted as the ability to "control your emotions." While emotional regulation is one component of self-regulation, the more accurate definition is actually much broader: the ability to stop, think, and make a choice about how to behave. Self-regulation spills over into almost all observable areas of a student's classroom patterns.

A child with strong self-regulation can:

- speak at an appropriate volume for the situation.
- remember and execute daily routines.
- take turns when playing a game, and remember the turn-taking order.
- put their belongings away in the appropriate location.

And, in contrast, a child with weaker self-regulation will often:

- blurt out answers and interrupt.
- speak loudly even when the room is quiet.
- need frequent reminders to follow daily routines.
- grab materials even when others are using them.
- lose track of whose turn it is, and/or grow impatient about having their turn in a game.
- lose track of their belongings.

These examples illustrate why self-regulation is so important in the early years of school. Strong self-regulation helps children have more positive peer relationships, and stronger connections to their teachers, which, in turn, are linked to stronger academic outcomes. Self-regulation extends to a child's ability to manage their own behavior as well as how they display and express their emotions.

Emotional Regulation

You will notice that we did not say that self-regulation is what allows a child to **control** their emotions. The fact is, none of us – child or adult – can really choose or therefore control the existence of our emotions. What we are able to control (to varying degrees, depending on context) is how we display and express our emotions. If we are frustrated by something that is shared in a staff meeting, we can feel frustrated, while choosing not to show that frustration at the time. We may choose to vent later on to a friend, or sneakily send an eye-roll emoji to a colleague; these strategies are actually excellent examples of strong emotional regulation! When supporting young children in regulating their emotions, it is important to deeply grasp that the goal is not to squelch the emotions themselves, but rather to choose safe and pro-social ways to display and express those emotions.

A child with strong emotional regulation can:

- identify their own feelings and/or emotional state.
- select a strategy to manage their emotions.

Some examples of this:

- seeking comfort from an adult when upset or distressed
- verbally expressing hurt feelings to a classmate

Behavioral Regulation

The inevitable and essential complement to emotional regulation is behavioral regulation: a child's ability to manage and select behaviors that are appropriate to their context and likely to achieve their desired outcome. This also refers to their ability to suppress behaviors that may be inappropriate, unsafe, or ineffective.

A child with strong behavioral regulation can:

- remember a rule or expectation that applies to their behavior.
- adapt their behavior accordingly.

Some examples of this:

- walking, rather than running, in the hallway.
- raising their hand and waiting to speak.

The Importance of Co-regulation

If you have ever held a fussy infant, you know: as soon as that agitated, squirmy, screaming baby is taken out of the arms of a frazzled, frantic, sleep-deprived parent, and held snugly and securely by someone who is calm and relaxed, that baby will start to settle down. This scenario is the epitome of co-regulation: an adult sharing their calm with an out-of-control, completely dysregulated, tiny human. Children need co-regulation long past infanthood. In a classroom, you are the co-regulator! All of the routines you have put in place, and the physical environment you have created, will also support children's self-regulation.

When a child's emotions (and consequently, their behavior) are truly out of control, and they are caught in a whirl of sadness or anger, they are not able to settle by themselves. They need your help to get to a calmer and more focused place; your job right now is to share your calm. Like that tiny infant, they may benefit from reassuring touch, and may need to be held or hugged. Other ways to co-regulate a child who is in distress:

- taking a slow walk together
- humming or singing softly
- holding their hand
- rubbing their back
- offering a drink of water

The Role of Play in Self-Regulation

While there are specific games to support self-regulation (We like the book *Stop, Think, Act*, by Megan Mcclelland and Shauna Tominey for an in-depth look at self-regulation in the early childhood classroom), the most powerful tool to develop skills in this area is the thing children naturally want to do – PLAY! Here again, we see that children naturally want to engage in and repeat behaviors that ARE ACTUALLY TEACHING THEM THINGS! Naturally! It's not a chore to learn to walk or to engage in play, and neither of these is "goofing off"; rather, it's the work of a human child.

A child who is deeply engaged in play is automatically engaging their brain: planning tasks; persisting through difficulty; selecting and organizing materials; creating, following, and adjusting a plan; holding an idea in their head and adjusting their own actions in alignment with that idea. These are all components of executive functioning, and children can practice them without you needing to plan a specific lesson or intervention!

When it comes to self-regulation, dramatic play, where a child takes on a role and acts like someone different from themselves, is particularly powerful. When they take on the role of "parent" or "baby" or "kitten," a child then engages in sustained practice of regulating their own behavior in order to become someone else.

The green chapter of this book shares many more details about why play is the foundational element of a kindergarten classroom. For now, the important thing is that play builds young brains!

The Importance of Movement to Children's Development

Rapidly growing young children literally wake up to a new body every day. Just take a minute to think about that: can you as an adult even fathom what it might be like to literally have your arms, legs, and hands be CHANGING every day? Having your legs grow longer to the point where your pants are too short? It sounds so odd when you think of it in an adult context, but it is one of the most important kinds of work a child is doing from birth, for 18 years or so. The best and only way to understand a constantly changing body is to move that body and explore its capacities and limits. Again: if you woke up tomorrow, suddenly six inches shorter or taller, you would spend a great deal of time figuring out the things that you can now, or can no longer, do! You would also be pretty clumsy for a while as you adjusted to the change in your physical dimensions. Movement is a core skill and function in the early childhood classroom. All of this to say: your classroom should be fully equipped to support multiple types of (near constant!) movement.

Motor Skills in the Classroom

Developing children's core strength and gross motor skills:

- Make chairs optional. Rather than setting a chair at each spot, leave chairs piled at the edge of the room so chairs are opt-in rather than opt-out.
- Allow and encourage students to work while sitting on the floor or lying on their bellies.
- Keep your outside time sacred, and treat it with the same importance as math or literacy. While outside, encourage children to:
  - Jump off things (start small and work up to higher things): encourage them to stick the landing (similar to how a gymnast would, landing with bent knees and straightening up again). BONUS: they LOVE getting a "score" and performing for you – they will do this FOREVER – over and over again, all year long.
  - Play on the monkey bars: encourage them to hang on until a count of ten and then to beat their score. Increase difficulty by varying the height (again, start at the lowest settings and work up) and by having them hold their knees up or by doing a straddle.
  - Hang upside down. Sorry, we know this has sadly become a no-no in many school settings, but it is

essential work in both developing core strength and in literally helping kids orient in space. If your school doesn't allow this "trick," then encourage kids to sit inverted looking at the ceiling on chairs or couches at home, or even while just lying on the floor.

  - Practice their "tricks" (on the climbing structure, slide, swings, balance beams, and so on) while outside. Be prepared to hear your name 100,000 times as they shout "LOOK AT ME, TEACHER" over and over again. You will become a master at instantly manufacturing an enthusiastic facial expression and a sincere thumbs-up!
- Consider including scooters, Hula-Hoops, hopscotch in your classroom as part of your free play materials.
- Music, music, music! Keeping time to music matters!
- Make sure you allow for some type of movement activity or break every 15 minutes or so (oh yes, that much!)
- Work to incorporate physical movement into daily routines as well as your STEM and reading programs as much as possible.
- Work to incorporate wheels, balls, pulleys, and levers into your STEM program.
- When planning your centers for the week, intentionally include activities that support gross motor development.

Developing children's fine motor skills:

- Actively teach any gaps in self-care skills: zippers, buckles, buttons, lacing, all work on fine motor skills in authentic and meaningful ways.

Pro tip: for zippers, the "pin" is a man and he has to get into the elevator for this all to work. You can usually feel the man get in there. The elevator won't work unless he's all the way in! :)

- Materials and activities that support fine motor skill practice:
  - tweezers and cotton balls,

- tongs
- eye droppers
- Play-Doh, plasticine, and Silly Putty
- ripping paper
- anything with beads and/or lacing
- clothespins
- squirt bottles
- pipe cleaners
- using scissors on different textures and materials
- dressing and undressing dolls, puppets, stuffed animals. (Barbie clothes require a special level of skill and persistence!)
- drawing on different surfaces – horizontal, vertical, slanted – and in different positions (sitting, standing, laying on their tummies, sides, backs)

There are a million ideas out there for fine motor centers! Make sure you always have several in your rotation!

An essential resource in the arena of movement and young children is *Moving Smart*, founded by Gill Connell from New Zealand. Along with several publications, they offer videos and coursework to help teachers understand the critical role movement plays in development in early childhood. Along with helpful checklists, games, and charts, they discuss key points including how managing balls and uneven terrain helps children learn to manage unpredictability. Their work has become even more relevant as children's playgrounds and environments have become more and more controlled to the point of being too safe. You can find their website at the end of this chapter.

Keeping Kids Moving, Even in Rigid or Restrictive Settings

Unfortunately, it must be acknowledged that many districts/schools/administrators do not understand or value the role of children's development as the essential foundation to their learning. These settings often expect young children to behave and learn in the same ways as much older students, and therefore believe that early learning classrooms should resemble their counterparts in middle school, with young children spending much of their day sitting still and working on highly structured academic tasks. As we write this in 2020, many classrooms that are normally very child-centered have had to restrict children's spontaneous movement as part of the efforts to mitigate the risks of the COVID-19 pandemic. Knowing that there are many possible reasons why educators may find themselves in need of creative ways to meet children's need for movement, here are a few suggestions:

- Keep supplies centrally located away from work tables/desks, so children must get up and walk to get scissors, glue, crayons, and so on.
- For art or craft projects, set up the materials as a "buffet," or in stations around the room.
- Provide direct instruction and demonstration at your carpet/meeting area, then have children move to tables/desks to do their work.
- Insert movement into your transition routines, that is, "do five jumping jacks before you get dressed for recess."
- Allow and encourage students to stand while working at their desks or tables, rather than sitting.
- If space allows, encourage students to lie on their bellies during circle time/whole group meetings.
- Keep recess as an essential part of your daily schedule, and organize your day so that children never miss a minute of it.
- If you live in a climate where indoor recess occurs frequently, use this time for active movement, not for quiet activities like coloring or movies. You can find children's yoga and fitness videos online!

Valuing Children Where They Are: Letting Five Be Five

There are few things that make us bristle more than the idea of "preparing" kids for the next grade level. Somewhere along the way this became a trend that we'd love to see disappear.

Childhood is not preparation for adulthood, kindergarten is not preparation for "real" school, and adulthood is not preparation for death! Viewing each stage of human development as "preparation" for the next stage keeps us from honoring the uniqueness of the current stage. Honoring where children ARE is a gift to them and all the world. As Amy has been known to say: "Kindergarten teachers are not prep cooks; we are executive chefs!" If you focus on offering a complete, well-rounded, developmentally appropriate, and positive kindergarten experience, your students will be ready for the following year.

Assessment Checklist: Is Your Classroom Developmentally Appropriate?

- Students have room and freedom to move freely through the space
- Students can easily access materials for work and play
- Students have daily opportunities for physical activity
- Students go outdoors every day
- Furnishings are appropriate to students' age and size
- There are classroom routines and rituals for meaningful milestones (birthdays, lost teeth)
- Dramatic play is included and valued as part of children's educational programming, with time and materials to support it.
- Schedule and routines allow for practice and development of independent self-care skills
- Adequate time is allotted for developmental needs such as eating and rest

References and Recommended Reading

Berk, L. (2017). *Child development* (9th ed.). Pearson

Brodie, K. (2019). *Schema, activities and learning opportunities.* [PDF document] https://kathybrodie.s3.amazonaws.com/Schema-Guidelines.pdf

Connell, G., & McCarthy, C. (2013). *A moving child is a learning child: How the body teaches the brain to think (birth to age 7)*. Free Spirit Publishing.

Copple, C., & Bredekamp, S. (Eds.). (2008). *Developmentally appropriate practice in early childhood programs serving children from birth through age 8* (3rd ed.). National Association for the Education of Young Children (NAEYC).

Education Scotland. (2020). Schemas: Learning through play. [PDF document] https://education.gov.scot/parentzone/Documents/nih058-Parentzone-Booklet.pdf

Harvard University, Center on the Developing Child. (2020). Executive function & self-regulation. https://developingchild.harvard.edu/science/key-concepts/executive-function/

McClelland, M., Cameron, C., Wanless, S., & Murray, A. (2007). Executive function, behavioral self-regulation, and social-emotional competence: Links to school readiness. *Contemporary perspectives on research in social learning in early childhood education*. 83–107. Information Age Publishing.

McClelland, M.M., & Tominey, S.L. (2015). *Stop, think, act: Integrating self-regulation in the early childhood classroom* (1st ed.). Routledge.

Morrison, F.J., Ponitz, C.C., & McClelland, M.M. (2010). *Self-regulation and academic achievement in the transition to school.* In S.D. Calkins & M.A. Bell (Eds.), *Human brain development: Child development at the intersection of emotion and cognition* (pp. 203–224). American Psychological Association.

Moving Smart. (2020). https://movingsmart.co.nz/.

4

Green: The Complexity of Play

Young children learn by playing, and if they are not playing, they are not really learning in a deep and lasting way. What does it really mean to play? How do you work it into your classroom without it feeling like utter chaos? (Hint: make peace with a little bit of chaos …) Even harder: how do you explain the role of play to colleagues, parents, and administrators?

Play Is Learning

Once a cornerstone of early childhood programs, play has been so systematically pulled out of so many programs that the freedom and right to play has become an issue of social justice. In many schools, especially those with high populations of low-income students, the drive and focus is to "catch up," sometimes implementing strict rules and methods and more "instructional" time. While children of low income may experience the drive for "grit" and "no excuses," high-income children are often pushed into the same rigid standards in the push to "excel."

In practice, these approaches do harm by taking away opportunities for children to grow in self-regulation and therefore, to develop socially, emotionally, and academically. Less time for play means less time for language, creativity, exploration, discovery, flexibility of thought, personal and community responsibility, leadership, and adaptation. Play should be the cornerstone of any program – early childhood or not! Adults think of "work" and "play" as separate things, but to children there is only play. When they do a worksheet, in their minds, at least at first, they are playing at school, doing "official" work. They feel fancy and in control. This is part of why some students want to do worksheets – what they are really doing is "playing" at being big kids at school!

Like potty training or learning to walk, when kids aren't interested, they're usually *not ready*. It means they are doing *other developmental work*. By nature, they are busy doing the work they are meant to do. Our job is to let them, observe them at work and play, and to help them find their gifts and become more of themselves. It's a reciprocal relationship. They will teach you what they need when you learn to listen and interpret their unspoken language.

Why Play Belongs in School

If any good came out of the COVID-19 global pandemic, it was showing humans what was really important in life. Being isolated in quarantine for months gave parents and teachers a jarring lesson about the importance of social dynamics in the daily life of young children.

It is not unusual to hear "but they can play at home" from parents when teachers broach the topic and the role of play in a classroom. How can we, as educators, respond to this objection? The point is valid: yes, a child can absolutely play at home and they are hopefully doing so in a rich, child-friendly environment full of diverse, dynamic experiences and equipment designed to enrich their lives. Of course, we know that is not the case for ALL children, even for families of considerable wealth and means. So the first response to this objection is: school is the place where people work together as a society to ensure a basic foundation of experiences for ALL children.

Second, and most importantly, while yes, children can play at home, there is an important difference between playing within the confines and safety of a child's personal family system and that child interacting with the rich and varied array of experiences offered by a classroom community. In the community of children at school, kids are given opportunities to discover and try out new behaviors and strategies, to adapt to new experiences and routines, and to apply that knowledge in new and interesting ways. The environment of school facilitates interactions among communities of children that directly results in a dynamic growth of a range of skills of the individual.

Last, when children play at school, it is in the company of a trained professional in the arena of teaching and learning with young children (that's you!) The knowledge, skill, and insight of a teacher should support, extend, deepen, and broaden the scope of children's play and the learning it inherently creates.

How to Respond to "School is for learning, children can play at home or after school"

1. School is the place where we work together as a society to ensure a basic foundation of experiences for ALL children.
2. Play facilitates dynamic interactions among communities of children, which directly results in sustained growth and promotes a wide range of essential skill development for each individual child.
3. As a teacher, you are a trained professional in the arena of child development and teaching and learning with young children. Your role is to design rich play experiences for children and to assist each child as they grow, explore, and learn.

Let's now take a deeper dive into what exactly that means and how you can continue to grow as a professional in this area.

How Play Is Learning

The work of Vivian Gussin Paley provides some of the richest research and most in-depth explanation of the importance of children's play in learning. Paley's work is an essential reference for your professional collection of resources.

Pure play is unscripted and rapidly changing. It is a world of pretend that is dynamic and unplanned. It is an abstract community construct that is being created, demolished, and recreated with lightning speed. It is the breathless co-creation of dreaming up the impossible and the excitement of the possibility of making it all come to life. It is the joyful, soothing sensation of recreating familial daily life played out over and over again. Play is the art form and lifeblood of human development.

Your role as a teacher:

1. recognizing the value and critical importance of play in children's lives
2. protecting play and allowing children the space to play freely
3. enhancing and maximizing the classroom environment to allow for more play
4. observing and interpreting
5. advocating for play in school and committing to ongoing reading and research on the topic

One of the things we often forget to do as practitioners is to actually get on the floor and play with the children. Oftentimes, adults do this in an "instructional" way or in a way that is invasive and off-putting. Try not to approach play as an adult in charge. This is their game and their world. If you listen enough to learn to follow the unspoken rules, you just might gain an invitation to participate!

What Does It Mean to Play? True Play versus "Playful Work"

True play has no tangible or desired outcome other than fun. As teachers, we often try to harness that spirit and add tasks or desired outcomes to children's play. This can be a remarkable tactic with big payoffs – or it can squelch children's creativity and enthusiasm. While it is possible to "nudge" children's authentic play to include academic skills, this must be done delicately, in such a way that children believe it was their own idea.

Consider a school day when a group of children have turned the housekeeping area into a restaurant. You get the idea to add menus to their play to add some literacy skill development. If you walk into their play area with a stack of construction paper and markers announcing that their restaurant needs menus, you have just co-opted their authentic play into your work. If, on the other hand, you become part of the action, asking what they are serving or to see the menu, they will likely come up with the idea themselves and will soon be asking you for paper and writing materials, of their own accord.

"Free Play" Does Not Mean Chaos (and How to Spot the Difference)

A healthy and playful classroom environment should be a busy and bustling place with space for both quiet and active areas.

Many adults and even educators mistakenly equate "free play" with "all hell breaking loose." If the class is in complete chaos during play, it means either the community has not been sufficiently established or the class hasn't been exposed to enough opportunities to engage in free play. While play happens naturally, a peaceful and purposeful classroom doesn't occur by magic. It takes your hard work and commitment to establish a classroom community.

> *"One particularly difficult class that I timed at having altercations literally every 20 seconds had me halting everything as I had children sit down right where they were, no matter what they were doing and sit silently for a minute. If anyone started talking, the minute would start again until we collectively made it through. Achievable but ultimately not fun, it helped make the class more aware of themselves as they worked together to avoid the "penalty box." Textbook solution? No, but it worked."*
>
> *– Heidi*

Observing and Interpreting Free Play

As you gain experience working with young children within the same age groups, you'll notice more subtle patterns of play emerge year after year. After a full exploration of the world of toys, sound, and movement in preschool, by five and six years old children are working to appear more grown up and shed that "little kid stuff" in favor of carrying around a copy of *War and*

TABLE 4.1

A chaotic versus a balanced classroom

Chaotic	*Balanced*
Kids aren't certain where things belong or how to use the room, with (non-storage) areas left unused or accessible.	The class can tell any visitor about each area of the room and how it works.
As soon as the teacher turns her back, trouble begins. Kids are looking to see if the teacher is looking.	The teacher can lean out of the room for a minute or have a conversation with a colleague and nothing much changes.
It's loud and wild. Children might act fresh, mischievous, or "class clownish" to take leadership of the class.	It's loud and wild at times, but the teacher can transition the class from loud and wild to quiet and on the rug very smoothly and quickly.
Teacher is largely unaware of what's happening around the room.	Teacher is generally aware of what's happening in every corner of the room even if it might look like she's not paying attention.
Teacher is frenetic; frequently shouts or threatens, constantly moving boundaries and penalties to the class.	Teacher can raise an eyebrow or speak nonverbally to class to communicate boundaries.
The class has learned that the teacher is largely irrelevant or not dependable.	The class respects and admires the teacher.

Peace, matter-of-factly pointing out to poor Joey that, "Oh yes, I can read it, it's my favorite book."

By March, many kindergartners are becoming more deeply involved in what might be termed "airplay" – meaning the toys of the classroom are no longer the focus of children's play, and have become props to facilitate the breathless, joyful dance of collective imaginative play. This type of play is frequently unobserved or overlooked by the untrained eye. Watch for it! Of course you will have onlookers and those who prefer to learn by observing; they are watching groups of children rapidly fold in and out, as leaders spontaneously shift and change. It becomes a seeming tangle of chaos that everyone somehow understands except for you. Congratulations. Your class has officially hit a "sweet spot!"

DO NOT INTERRUPT: Signs You've Hit a Sweet Spot

Cat and baby play! This will start early in the year, with cries that may be meowing or pretend crying. Ask the kids and they will reluctantly tell you it's a baby mermaid cat – reluctantly, because they still aren't sure if they're *really* allowed to do this in school, and also because honestly, they'd really prefer it if you left.

When you hear the cats and babies come out, it's your cue to exit stage left and pretend you don't hear any of it. Of course, you can choose to surprise them at the circle later when they least expect it with, "Now, kittens, fold your paws, it's time for a story." They will be eating out of your hand in no time.

Speaking of pretend, around January, you'll start to hear "bertend" (pretend). By March, try to keep a tally of how many times you hear the word "bertend" in a minute. You will stop soon as you will likely hear this word 30 times a minute from different groups. The children are so excited by the sheer POSSIBILITY of it all coming to life that they just can't contain themselves. "Bertend, bertend, bertend." There are no toys involved except maybe a chair or a wand as a prop. It's all done "in the air" and looks like a strange, joyful, chaotic, and cooperative dance. They won't notice you watching, until they do and are shocked and slightly embarrassed. This is when you "bertend" not to notice and kindly leave them be.

Superhero and Fantasy Play

What used to be "Cops and Robbers," is now superheroes who have taken over the airwaves of childhood and become the go-to for fantasy play. Superheroes have magical powers as their weapons of choice, which may be an improvement over toy guns, but still causes worry for some adults about the role of violence in children's play. There is a wealth of research confirming that good versus evil play is important to children's growing understanding of the world, and provides an important outlet for them to explore concepts of power/control, right versus wrong, and life/death. The role of fantasy is important as children imagine themselves as powerful and capable combatants against dark forces.

Understanding and Interpreting Play: Essential Researchers and Writers

Vivian Gussin Paley

Vivian Gussin Paley's work and writing is largely centered around the importance of storytelling and play both in children's lives and in the classroom. One of our favorite suggestions from Paley is that you try to write down the dialogue of an imaginative play scene while it's in action. It is next to impossible as it becomes almost breathless with dynamism, morphing and changing faster than you could hope to write. Paley's extensive body of work is a must-read for any early childhood educator. Add her to your summer reading list!

Karen Wohlwend, Ph.D.

Karen Wohlwend, PhD, author of *Literacy Playshop,* is a professor at Indiana University Bloomington who studies the impact of toys, play, and imaginative storytelling on literacy and language development. Her work centers around how toys provide essential language development and how media and literacy helps facilitate connections among children.

For some reason it's an accepted practice to ban children's personal toys from coming into school. Perhaps this was one of those things that started back in 1983 and just became such an accepted practice that no one questioned it. While toys can get lost at school, you can also use the bringing in of items from home as a discussion point and help children begin to make choices and decisions for themselves. As you start to allow dolls and toys to come into the classroom, you will be amazed at how those once banned personal items really do facilitate social interactions and language development. Dr. Wohlwend's research shows that children's toys and play are essential to literacy development and help provide a vehicle for children to connect and share with each other, all while seamlessly fostering literacy skills.

Lilian Katz, PhD

A legendary leader and author of over 100 publications on issues surrounding early childhood education, Katz's work centers not so much on the specific role of play, but more around children's "learning dispositions" and how the structure and questions teachers ask children while immersed in the process of learning affects children's learning. Her work is an essential piece of the play puzzle as she discusses and breaks down the inquiry process children go through when approaching learning. She asks us to think about year-long constructivist projects like "All About Balls" or "Things That Attach" versus doing abstract units like "Dinosaurs" or "The Rainforest." Dr. Katz shows how logical, well-placed questions, active experimentation, and discovery along with ongoing discussion impacts the learning life of young children. You will definitely want this expert in early learning and the project approach on your bookshelf!

Defending Play

When you teach young children for any length of time, you can be sure one day you will be faced with defending the role of play. Whether it be to a parent, colleague, administrator, family member, or the wider community, it is important you consider part of your job as an advocate for play in schools and its critical role in human learning, primarily because of the impact on the emotional and social lives of children, but also because research tells us play has a *direct impact* on young human academic life as well. Play is an issue of social justice and is included in the UN Convention on the Rights of the Child.

Self-Regulation

Self- regulation forms the cornerstone of your argument as to why play is important. It is also an easily hijacked term as people often misuse it interchangeably with "self-control." Self-control and self-regulation are very different things , however, and it is important that you can distinguish between the two.

Self-regulation is the overall skill of being able to gauge and adapt to changing social interactions, cope with changing circumstances, and modify behaviors in order to achieve a goal. Self-regulation is primarily built through playing with other children in unscripted settings. The act of free play is essentially children literally practicing and experiencing adapting to frequently changing dynamic scenarios among peers.

Self-control occurs more at the moment of an instance of resistance to oblige an urge. You exhibit self-control when you resist a purchase or an extra piece of pie. It's self-regulation that prevents you from lying down on the floor and crying about it.

How Play Supports Self-Regulation

When we take free play out of schools and classrooms, we take away the opportunity for children to become better self-regulators. Dynamic play requires little Paulina to make adjustments when Carla tells her she can't be the mother. No one has ever told Paulina "no" before as she has primarily played house alone at home or with her mom or dad. It may stun poor Paulina at first, but in fact it is one of the best things that has ever happened to this young child as she is challenged as to what to do next. Does she start crying immediately? You will definitely encounter that! Does she hit Carla? You will encounter that as well! Or does she adapt and turn into a sister or a dog? Does she walk away and start her own game? While children's strong self-regulation skills often go undetected, those who struggle are definitely noticed as they often express the frustration of the challenge of adapting to free-play scenarios.

As free play is the exact time that children who exhibit lower self-regulation skills struggle, it is also the time when kindergarten drama unfolds in its most unpleasant and tiresome form. However exasperating it can be to deal with these seemingly miniscule and constantly repeated issues, it is the primary work of the young child, and absolutely critical for them, to be engaged in practicing facing obstacles and handling adjustments. Be proactive and expect these situations to arise. Conducting short, 15-minute, 100 percent observations of a child at play can help you better target their needs. Read up on behavior and classroom management in the Blue chapter to help you put a plan in place.

Ways to Sneak Play into a Rigid or Highly Scripted Setting

Even in the best settings, at some point you'll need to disguise "play" as "formal curricular work." This is where your room design is going to do a lot of the heavy lifting for you and why it's important to take the time to set up the room slowly and with purpose. Kids can be playing blocks during math and you whip out your "How Blocks Support Mathematics" card in a pinch. Or say the assignment is for children to work with "three-dimensional shape manipulatives" in order to explore architecture and physics. Spend a lot of time thinking about what your room is trying to teach. Your classroom design is going to do a lot of this work for you. Let's look at how you can maximize your room to allow for free play while fulfilling academic requirements.

Making Space: Setting It Up for Play

Philosophy of Design

Take a minute to contrast your idea of a welcoming early childhood setting with the starkness of the desks and walls of a high school classroom, and it becomes easy to understand how the role of the classroom may impact children and learners of all ages.

It's been interesting watching the aesthetics of classrooms change over the years. Years ago, the super happy rainbow-themed room had its day. Now it's woven baskets and neutral shades as new research on children's attention span has helped teachers tone things down. Over the years on Kinderchat, we've seen elaborate spaces that were fit for classroom design TV shows, humble trailers, rooms without windows, and completely outdoor classrooms. Whatever your situation, your job is to maximize the space for functionality, friendliness to children's needs, and to have the space be flexible enough to serve multiple functions.

Thinking of your classroom as a "house for children" is helpful; the kinder-garten is a "child's garden" – the name stuck for a reason! The design of an early childhood classroom is one of the most powerful learning tools out there. The MIT Lab that creates Scratch coding programs is called the "Lifelong Kindergarten," and uses the model of the early childhood classroom to help maximize a playful, creative approach to their work.

- Your room design will help you "differentiate" learning and address the wide varieties of abilities and needs of children.
- Your classroom should be doing a lot of your work for you and requires regular and ongoing and intentional thought, planning, and updating.

A well-designed early childhood classroom can accommodate any age or academic level of learner.

Just like a home, the classroom should have areas for living, having conversation, exploring, building, cooking, cleaning, eating, working, playing, doing projects, and resting. In early childhood, let movement lead and the children's experimentations and constructions be your guide. Allow music its full breadth as an essential foundational component to reading. (And kindly forgive these authors as we are fully aware how loud a child-led rhythm section can get!)

Good room design requires you to constantly push yourself to think about what you are really trying to teach and what any subject matter *actually means. What is reading really? What are the essential components of learning letters? Of discerning line and shape?* We encourage you to not segment your room into high school subject matters, but to construct a room design that meets the developmental needs of young children.

Keep Centers Moving and Changing

Young children's attention spans are SHORT. Even when fully focused and engaged, play scenarios change and morph rapidly. No matter how beautiful your room is, after four to six weeks it needs a refresher. Moving things around also helps your own mind to not get too settled into a routine, to help you think about

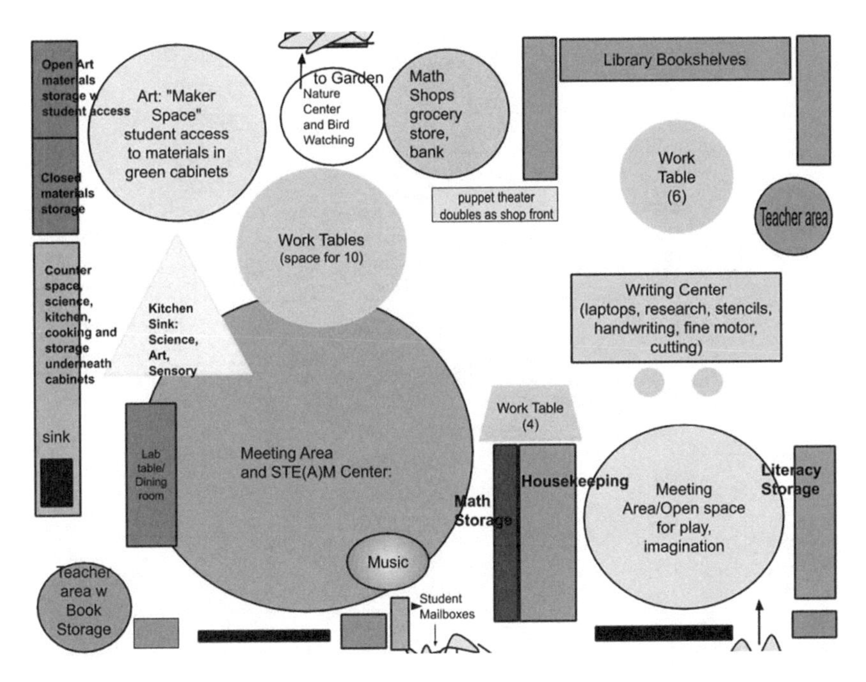

FIGURE 4.1
Sample room design

your space, and to change what's not working. Even a small change can have a big impact!

Rearranging your room every four to six weeks helps everyone gain a fresh perspective and keeps projects moving.

Follow the Kids' Interests

Most importantly, LISTEN to children. They are the users of your room and will tell you what's working and what they need. No, not with words – anything but! They will tell you through their actions, through their arguments with other children, through what's getting heavy use, and through what's left undiscovered and used. *Listen* to how they play and work, and design accordingly. That doesn't mean frantically jumping up to change things around at children's every whim; instead, it means staying one or two steps ahead and anticipating where the play wants to go and making space for it to happen.

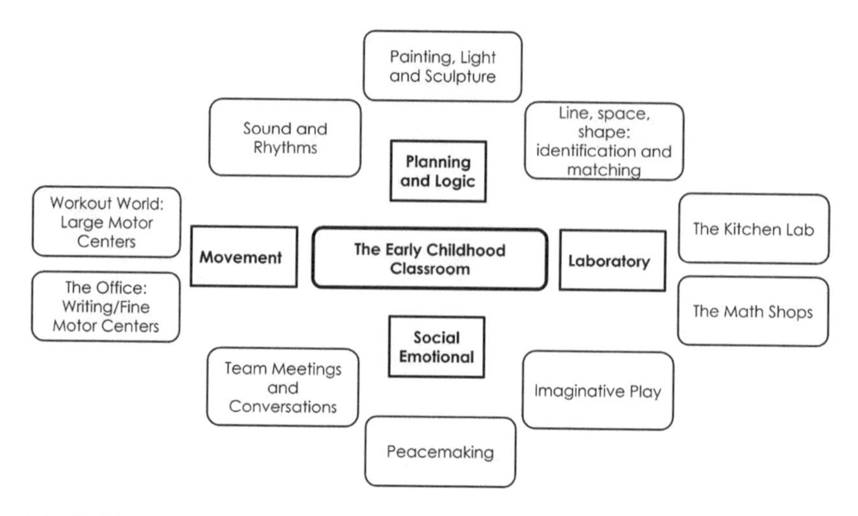

FIGURE 4.2
Popular center ideas

Popular Center Ideas

Centers to Foster Social-Emotional Development

Imaginative play areas:

The room should have smaller spaces for quiet imaginary play, places for children to interact with toys and each other, as well as open space where their imaginations can take full reign. Having designated spaces allows you to "open" some areas and "close" others. Doing this helps prevent overuse, too many choices, and encourages children to branch out and try other centers they may not be as drawn to.

One of the saddest things to see in early education is rooms young children without multiple spaces for imaginative play. Young children rely on toys to help give voice to their imagination. Your room should have a wide variety of toys to help children expand social narratives, encourage language development, and ground their emotional selves.

> *"I have always felt like my best teacher-self when my role has essentially been reduced to 'prop provider.'"*
>
> *– Heidi*

The word "props" is interesting here, as in stage props that help foster a storyline. "Props" is short for "property." This is exactly what your class will likely spend a majority of time fighting over. Though tempting to blame, it's usually not the fault of not having enough of a toy or prop; rather, it's the developmental work of the age to fight over "property." Young children have been exerting developmental control over "property" since they could say "mine," and they continue to engage in that work throughout early childhood. The fighting and arguing that will inevitably take place over toys and props is actually helping foster conversation, dialogue, problem-solving, and self-regulation.

Having a wide variety and changing array of props and toys will help minimize arguments, but be prepared for them, they will occur – we guarantee that with a 100 percent accuracy rate. That leads to why your peacemaking center is such a key space in any classroom, but especially in a classroom designed for young children. Follow their lead, listen to what they are playing, and add materials as needed.

Peacemaking/feelings center (problem-solving, leadership, empathy, and emotional growth):

This is where your knowledge, preparation, and experience come in as you've anticipated the issue and are ready for the inevitable showdown with a system in place: the Peacemaking Center.

Your peacemaking or "feelings area" should be tucked in enough to allow for a range of emotions to rage with some degree of privacy for the child, while ensuring teacher visibility. *In the beginning, you will need to work hard to apply the structure of this center to help children understand how it works.* As this center primarily gets used at the time of meltdowns or issues, it might take anywhere from a few weeks or a few months before it becomes part of the culture and practice of your classroom. Refer to Chapter Blue for more specifics on facilitating dialogue in this center. Some of our classes have logged long hours in the peacemaking area, while other years it's gone largely unused. In either case, being ready with a strategy for handling upsets and arguments will save you (and them!)

Props:

- dialogue chairs
- sandpaper and sticks
- puppets
- feelings books
- labeled pictures or photographs of a range of feelings expressions
- weighted stuffed animal or blanket
- squeeze balls
- tissues

Team Meetings and Conversations (community, literacy):
It's fun to think of your meeting area as a "team meeting space" or a space for conversation instead of your "direct instruction" space. Will you do any "direct instruction" here? Sure, but it doesn't have to feel so strict and buttoned up. Your class might not start out as a team, but they will become one! Whether you are leading a math team meeting or having a social-emotional problem-solving session led by puppets, your team needs ample place to gather. This is where everyone checks in, and shares. This space also doubles nicely as a play space after meetings are over.

Props:

- full-year calendar
- birthday chart (can double as the calendar)
- daily schedule
- clock
- puppets
- access to audio and video
- space to write (easel, whiteboard)
- bin of current read-alouds so you are always ready to read

Centers to Foster Movement and Strength

Two favorite centers will work for you to help both fine and large motor skills.

"The Office" (fine motor, literacy):

Calling it a writing center is soooo fifth grade. "Writing center" carries enormous weight and expectation and limits the mind so that both teacher and student end up thinking it's a place to write the great American novel. Perhaps this is why "writing centers" often don't get used. Instead, try PLAYING AT WRITING. Little kids generally don't know what happens at an "office." It's an exotic place they've maybe heard of, and abstract enough to be enticing. Suddenly, they need to get to work. Add an old telephone and watch the orders pour in. What orders, you say? Doesn't matter. Use your handy-dandy pinkie and thumb phone to call in and place one!

Props:

- various types of paper and notepads
- pencils and pens
- an old telephone (get two if you can, trust us)
- stencils (alphabet, number)
- hole punchers
- staplers
- scissors
- tape
- an old keyboard or computer
- dictionary, atlas
- calculators (in a pinch, they can double as phones, plus all those orders might need to be added up someday!)

"Workout World" (large motor, math):

This center is the one that might get you into trouble with other teachers. Keep this one in your back pocket for rainy days or when the weather turns cold. It's one of those "centers in a bag" you can easily pack up and move around. "Workout World" is essentially a gym in a bag. One-two-three instructional illustrations of various movements help children match their bodies to the picture while working to count to 20 or do two sets of ten. (How many is that?!) Create a little circuit and watch them go!

(Note: It's the scooter that gets me in trouble with teachers as I often allow the scooter to be "open" during general playtimes. Something annoys teachers about kids rolling around on a scooter in the classroom! Thing is, nothing helps develop core strength quite like a scooter!) –Heidi

Props:

- beanbags, Hula-Hoops, jump ropes, scarves
- crawl-through tunnel
- scooters
- activity movement cards
- yoga cards
- balance teeters
- hands, feet, and directional arrows (trace, cut out, and laminate to use as guides)
- balls of various sizes
- timers

Centers to Develop Skills in Planning and Logic

These more unusual play centers may be ones you've never heard or thought of as essential to any classroom, but they do diligence and perform functions essential to a well-rounded, exploratory, and developmental curriculum. Along with creating vibrantly rich and imaginative worlds, children need anchors. In order to read, they need to be able to determine and follow rhythms, lines, and beats. They need experiences that teach them what kinds of things can physically stick together, what balances on what, and how things fit together. They are actively working to be able to discern line, pattern, and shape. These are all the prework and the basis of reading, but also of philosophy, logic, science, and mathematics. Even if you are lucky enough to have music or art class, these types of play activities are a must for any classroom.

Rhythm and sound center (literacy, coordination, patterns, executive functioning):

You can introduce and start using this as a teacher-led center with the "Eric Carle" project (see Chapter Orange). Your rhythm section can also form a "Birthday Band" of singers and shakers. While these are both examples of songs children know and play along with, it's also important to give them time to work with sound, patterns, and rhythms in an open-ended manner, aka PLAY.

The good news is that you can wait until the dreary days of bad weather come your way to introduce it as an option. The bad news is that IT WILL GET LOUD. Like REALLY LOUD. When you first open this center, of course they will fight over that ONE mysteriously special item. Then they will be LOUDLY out of sync for quite some time while they bang, shake, yowl, and sing. Some years, you might even be lucky enough to get a class that eventually syncs up. For some alternate and quieter uses, this area can also function as your team meeting center and technology area with a story listening center, keyboards, and music technology.

Props:

- egg shakers and rhythm sticks
- drums/homemade things that create percussion
- various musical instruments
- piano keyboard (SAY "OH YES" to plug-in earphones!)
- computer/iPad
- listening and sound equipment
- story listening center
- headphones and listening equipment

A note on story listening centers: unless the kids know how to change the (tape, CD, record, computer selection), they will need YOU TO DO IT. That means, if your story is six minutes long, you are over there every six minutes restarting it for the next group or changing the tape. To update, try creating collections of online books in "bins" in a Padlet. This, however, introduces quite a bit of technology, and you will need to teach how to access it step-by-step. You can visit Kinderchat.org to access our virtual classroom to see some examples.

Painting, shadow, and sculpture (experiencing the physical world, sensory, observation, visual discrimination, inventiveness):

Children love to design and create, and should have ample time to explore how paint colors mix together, how different brushes and textures interact with paint and various surfaces, and what elements balance and work together. If you have a sunny window or can get outside, explore light, shadows, reflections, water, and rainbows. There are numerous blogs and references with units on incorporating light tables and light projectors into your curriculum. Keep various craft supplies well stocked to allow the children to create sculptures and explore balancing and assembling objects and elements of design.

> *A note on craft supplies: As our planet earth faces environmental devastation largely due to human overconsumption of goods and materials, it is important that you do your part teaching children what constitutes materials suitable for creating their work. Those little foam pieces so popular now will be here for an eternity. Please ask yourself if there is really no other way you can create a project than by using googly eyes, pipe cleaners, foam pieces, or purchased items that aren't recyclable. Try to use found objects and sustainable items as much as possible in your work. You'll notice they look more attractive and are less expensive to supply as well!*

Props:

- paper towel rolls
- attractive cardboard boxes
- various types of paper; color construction, watercolor, large easel
- tape: Scotch, masking, and painter's
- paints: watercolor and tempera
- various types of brushes
- recycled washed yogurt cups to hold water or paints
- light projector
- flashlights
- water beads
- colored glass or see-through materials
- cloth to make spaces dark

Line, space, shape (visual discrimination, patterns, 1:1 correspondence, literacy, math, decision making, observation): Can you "read" a shell, rock, or leaf? Absolutely! And when you "read" it carefully, it tells you its name! Wait, leaves talk? Of course they do! They want to tell you the name of the tree family they belong to! You can only learn that by digging deep, studying their shape and qualities, and working to make a match. That's a big part of what scientists do.

Acknowledging that kids need experience, space, and time to explore concepts of space, shape, and line opens up so many possibilities for this center, which can hold your block and building areas as well.

Matching and Identification Area

This center can appear and disappear as needed, depending on the time of year and unit of study, but you should have a sequence in mind of things the kids can work to identify by using reference materials to identify types of shells, leaves, rocks, birds, plants, herbs, and so on.

Props:

- leaf and plant sorting and identification center
- bird watching and identification center
- rocks and minerals matching and identification center
- collections of various signs and symbols (road, environmental print, technology)
- sorting boxes
- magnifying glasses
- binoculars
- pencils and paper
- field guides
- puzzles
- pattern blocks
- nuts and bolts

Blocks (Relevant in Every Academic and Social-Emotional Area!)

Your blocks area is one of the most valuable and often underutilized areas in the early childhood classroom. Whole

Name:____________________
Draw your building:

What shape blocks did you use?
How many blocks did you use in your building? _____

FIGURE 4.3
Sample form for blocks

books have been written on blocks, and we encourage you to do ongoing work and research into how they are essential and applicable to multiple areas of your curriculum. Check out professional development opportunities from the "City and Country School" in New York City, for their blocks program that started in 1913 and is now known throughout the world. You can also add a "form" for kids to fill out. Some will work with more than others, but you can use it as a formal "math lesson" or center to help disguise play (see: "ways to disguise play").

Props:

- blocks set, storage, and space to create (ideally lasting) structures
- pencils and paper for drawing structures
- camera for photographing and documenting
- architectural drawings and books
- characters, action figures, natural materials, or dollhouse furniture
- This area can also serve as a shop with screwdrivers, hammers, and nails when you are ready to open the woodshop center. A woodshop area can fit in multiple other locations of your classroom as well, depending on the functionality of your space.

Laboratory

Children need to explore, "do," experiment and play with academic concepts and materials to help them gain experience and familiarity with the things they are being asked to learn. Identifying and counting coins on worksheets is very different from the act of handling money in a bustling café. Children need the opportunity to engage in experiences related to the real world.

The math shop (working with money or representations of money, economics, trade, counting):

This is a staple center and helps form the "Banking" or "Shop" section of your little classroom neighborhood. Different from the Office, the "Shops" should change into a bank, post office, and various stores of the children's own choosing and invention. This is your "math in action" station where the children can play with money and counting tools. It often just becomes the "Money Store" and that's just fine.

The trick to this station is to resist the temptation to exert control and enforce too many academic concepts and practices. Nothing kills play like too many rules and teacher control. Balance is key. Follow the kids' lead – it should all feel like their own idea. Who would have thought a well-placed pretend cash register would lead to the invention of a Money Store? What a great idea! Trays, signs, and the right prop at the right time can infuse structure into the play. Start with minimal materials and watch to know when it's the right time to add new materials.

Props:

- old telephone
- calculators
- play cash register
- play money (layer in, don't overwhelm with choice, match to your curriculum)
- clocks
- time cards and order forms
- calendars
- Unifix sorting trays
- counting tools

The Kitchen Lab: Sensory Science

Another center generally unpopular with adults and yet wildly popular with kids is the "Kitchen Lab" center. The closest we usually get to this center is sensory water tables or "cooking" where the work is super controlled, that is, "OK, now who wants to put the teaspoon of salt in the mix?" Everyone desperately raises their hands or waits to be called on to carefully take the spoon from the teacher's hand, handle it for three seconds, and return to their spot, waiting for the next opportunity to be the chosen one.

While cooking in a group from a recipe has its place, it's a missed opportunity for scientific exploration to not utilize a "kitchen lab" as a place for children to make their own mixes and discoveries. Teachers in the United Kingdom do much of this work outdoors through their famous "mud kitchens." The same idea can be applied inside and with various ingredients and materials to promote both sensorial experiences and scientific discoveries.

You don't need an actual kitchen to make this center happen. It can be as simple as a water table or just a table, and props and tools appear when needed. This center can easily move around, starting and ending outside, should you have the access or have it open at various times throughout the days of dreary weather. Proceed through a series of elements: water, solids, mixings, dough, temperature, weights, balances, and the physics of water! But don't forget the sensorial fun of a good old-fashioned mess making.

Props:

Liquids:

- water table, buckets, or deep and wide trays
- sponges
- turkey basters
- pitchers and pouring
- paintbrush (for "painting" outside with water on surfaces)
- colored water for color mixing and dyes (this can be a mess but definitely a good unit)
- paper towels and eyedroppers of colored water

- soap (for alternately a bubble unit or laundromat or car wash play)
- water tubes (physics unit)
- changing states of water
- sink and float unit

Solids:

- clay or Play-Doh and the tools to cut, shape (the changing shapes of solids)
- outdoor mud kitchen with mud and dirt
- liquids' impact on
- yeasts and doughs
- weights and balances
- temperature effects on (freezing and melting)
- seeds and gardening unit (grow, harvest, and make salads; harvest marigold seeds; sort and categorize seeds)

While young children can learn about gases through different experiments, it's still something they can't actually see or touch. Yes, you can do the balloon bit, and of course it's possible to "do it," but generally we recommend leaving this aspect for older children.

Nuts and bolts: Entryways and Exits

Of course, keep clear for fire, but entryways and exit systems should also help students form and reinforce daily routines and habits.

Cubbies and Coat Rooms

Whether your cubbies are outside the room or inside the classroom, they should be located near the entrance to your room. The cubbies are a transitional space much like the entryway to a home and should be designed for heavy use, including handling mud, snow, changes of clothing, and storage of lunches and backpacks.

Cubby areas bridge the space between home and school, and require efficiency and regular, ongoing management. My first mentor would include a drawing for parents of how the shoebox she wanted them to bring in should be organized. While you don't have to be quite that dedicated to them, you should have your class regularly clean them out. You don't want to learn the hard way and find liquified sushi in one at the end of the year as we once had the pleasure of discovering.

Having children do regular cubby maintenance helps teach organizational skills and gives children ownership and responsibility in maintaining their space.

Folders/Notes Coming to and from School

Your home notes and folders area is like your mail center at home and requires both upkeep and accessibility. It should be located near the exit or entrance to your classroom and should be set up for independent student management as much as possible. With increased use of technology, there's definitely less paper coming back and forth from school and home, but it's still a factor you should plan for. For older grades, this would be your homework station – though, while we're discussing this, Kinderchat's official position is that homework is not recommended for elementary-aged students.

Storage Areas

You'll always need more, but that's also your cue to purge. Closed storage areas are a godsend as they keep your room looking tidy when it's anything but. Keep it a goal to have your "behind closed doors" storage spaces organized and ready for full view at any time. As someone who has inherited and had to sort and purge many former teachers' stashes of files and materials, it can take some time to get these spaces in order, but doing so will help you function more efficiently.

Work Tables

In designing a room, most people start with the tables first. Instead, try thinking of the tables LAST. Don't let them be the boss of your room. While kids need places to work, they will rarely be working all at once together. Creating different nooks and areas for work seats helps keep them from dictating the design of your room and allows for more focused small-group work. I always red=flag a classroom where work tables are the dominant feature in the room. It shows that kids are largely doing seat work instead of actually USING the room and space.

Outdoor Play

Outdoor play is one of the most important aspects of any quality early childhood program. We highly recommend tracking down "Forest Kindergarten" videos and watching and learning from these fully immersive outdoor schooling experiences. What's most interesting about these school experiences is how children are expected to be independent and to persist through difficulty. Too often we only expect children to persist through a worksheet, while never giving them the opportunity to do physical work, which is the primary way children learn and experience the world. It is our job as educators to ensure that children experience the out-of-doors regularly, each day and for extended time periods and in all kinds of weather.

As children are asked to do more and more academic, indoor learning, they are losing skills that are critical to being environmentally aware, spatially oriented, and physically agile. Increasingly, we see children missing enough core strength to even sit up for lengths of time.

How many children and adults cannot name the type of trees that surround their school or neighborhood? Without trees, we cannot breathe. Surely it is important to acknowledge them? How many children think peacocks are native to their town? Can they name five birds that they might see in their neighborhood? Knowing your environment *is a literacy.* Sadly, most children and adults have become illiterate in the language of nature to the point where we are in a global crisis. As a teacher, YOU have the power to change the world by making sure children are grounded in the natural world versus artificial spaces. Get your kids out there, enjoying and learning about the natural world around them.

Outdoor education is not only important for science but also for the child's own physical well-being. Outside of the well-known benefits of the outdoors having positive effects on social-emotional well-being, ADHD, trauma, and stress, time outdoors helps children orient themselves to the natural world and builds unique muscle memory required for physical sturdiness. Climbing on rocks and navigating the uneven surfaces of the natural world far surpasses the predictability of the plastic playground.

Risky Play, Challenge and Risk Assessment

The sound of outdoor "risky play" usually makes teachers nervous. No teacher wants to get sued or ever be responsible for a child being seriously injured. Allowing children to engage in making risk assessment is very different than being irresponsible. Spend a lot of time watching children and you notice that they generally pause before taking that extra big jump. They rethink it, go down a step, or take a big breath and GO FOR IT! Of course, there's always that one kid who either purposefully falls (for the drama – he can't resist!) or for lack of skill. If it's a lack of skill in a reasonable task, he should be able to try it again and again until he is successful, or to have you step in and break down the goal into more achievable steps. Kids want to be physically challenged over and over again, and with increased difficulty. If you are having a lot of behavioral issues, this is likely why: *they are not being physically challenged enough.*

Children need to be PHYSICALLY WORKING, and too often we've constrained them where they don't have enough space or freedom to move and learn. This is especially true for children of color, who disproportionately face unequal expectations of behavior and often endure "rigorous" academic programs without adequate time for play and movement. Play is one of the leading issues of social justice that largely goes undetected as children are forced to try to "catch up" through developmentally inappropriate educational programs, all while being deprived of the exact types of learning experiences that will help them thrive.

We have to both trust and teach children to make reasonable assessments of what is safe for them. So many teachers are terrified of a kid picking up a stick, yet will give her a ruler. *What does that teach a child about the world?*

You will most certainly encounter a child who desperately wants to be doing things that are too hard for him. That child needs you! Help him save face by giving your attention to a simpler task you know he can do and praising that activity, slowly scaffolding in variations. Jump from a lower level, but land it perfectly with bent knees and then stand up. Or try a split jump from the same level. That child who is overassessing his ability to navigate risk needs you to teach and guide him as he learns to negotiate his pride and ability. This is real teaching!

> *"Risk-benefit assessment means that the provider considers two goals alongside each other: the goal of protecting children from avoidable serious harm, and the goal of providing them with stimulating, adventurous play opportunities."* – Play Scotland

Play Scotland has excellent resources on risky play; Scotland in particular has extensive information on this subject and is a global leader in developing play curricula. Kierna Corr (@CiarnaC on Twitter) blogs regularly about her work outdoors at Learning for Life, and Rob Ridley (@RangerRidley) is another wonderful resource who is the coordinator for the Outdoor Education Centers at the Peel School district in Ontario, Canada. Longtime Kinderchat moderator and contributor Carrie Marshall (@ carriemarshall1 on Twitter) has been working to complete a series of teacher certifications from *National Geographic*. Wherever you are in the world, there are resources waiting for your discovery!

How to Incorporate Outdoor Learning in Any Setting

Outdoor learning is more difficult to achieve and access in some settings more than others. While some schools may have access to parks, forests, or plentiful natural spaces, others have extremely limited access. If you have limited access, it's time to get creative.

- Take daily walks in the neighborhood around your school.
- Convert an unused area into a more natural space for exploration.
- Add plants into your room, turn off the lights, put animal sounds on, and simulate the out-of-doors each day for quiet time.
- Find a local park, natural space, or nature organization and build an ongoing relationship with them.
- Set up a bird-watching station by the window and/or stream the free Cornell bird cams on your smartboard or computer.
- Stream various animal cams and nature scenes throughout the day.
- Work to increase the natural space around your school as an issue of social justice. The well-being of children and the community depends on more green spaces!
- Have a space where children can dig deep using real shovels.
- Plan for each child to plant trees each year!

Assessment Checklist: Free Play

Use this checklist to guide your observations of each student's participation, engagement, and confidence during free play.

- How does (name) fare during unstructured play? Are they looking to the teacher for direction? Lost? Engaged with peers?
- Does (name) need teacher assistance to break into groups? Find a project?
- What kinds of things does (name) most gravitate toward?
- What is (name's) latest project or interest?
- What kinds of questions are you asking (name) to forward their thinking?
- Describe how (name) works in groups.
- What centers does (name) tend to avoid?

- What are common arguments and how does (name) fit into those?
- What is (name) like during outdoor play times?
- Does (name) take responsible risks? Describe their newest outdoors challenge and accomplishment

References and Recommended Reading

Ball, D., Gill, T., & Spiegal, B. (2012). *Managing risk in play provision: Implementation guide.* National Children's Bureau. playscotland.org/resources/print/Managing-Risk-in-Play-Provision-implementation-guide-2nd-edition-3.pdf?plsctml_id=11515

City and Country School. (n.d.). *Blocks program.* www.cityandcountry.org/programs/blocks-program

Corr, K. (2011–2020). *Learning for life.* https://nosuchthingasbadweather.blogspot.com.

Echternacht, H. (2013, June 2). *Stream: Play, life, love and literacy: The early childhood classroom.* https://hechternacht.wordpress.com/tag/room-design/

Katz., L.G., & Helm, J.H. (2000). *Young investigators: The project approach in the early years.* Teachers College Press.

National Geographic. (2020). *Educator certification.* www.nationalgeographic.org/education/professional-development/educator-certification/

Paley, V. G. (2004). *A child's work: The importance of fantasy play.* The University of Chicago Press.

Resnick, M. (2017). *Lifelong kindergarten: Cultivating creativity through projects, peers, passion and play.* The MIT Press.

Ridley, R. (2013–2020) *Epiphanies in environmental education: Curriculum beyond the classroom.* https://rangerridley.wordpress.com.

United Nations. (1989). Convention on the Rights of the Child. *Treaty Series, 1577*, 3.

Wohlwend, Karen. (2014). *Literacy playshop.* Teachers College Press.

5

Blue: Behavior and Classroom Management

If a kindergarten classroom often feels like a circus (and, let's be real: IT DOES FEEL LIKE A CIRCUS), how do you become an expert ringmaster? The process started four chapters ago, with routines and relationships, but there are also specific things you can do every day to keep the elephants in formation so everyone stays safe and is able to perform at their best.

The Basics of Classroom Management

First, you will notice we called this chapter **classroom** management, and not **behavior** management. There is a reason for this! Behaviors belong to individual children, while a classroom includes everyone (teachers, too!) as well as the physical environment. While every class will have at least one (and often more) individual child whose behavior needs support, if the classroom is well managed, the behaviors will be reduced. (Don't worry, we have several pages about behavior, too, coming right up!)

It's Not Them, It's You

To the untrained eye, a room full of five-year-olds is a chaotic place, and this is even more true in a classroom that is developmentally appropriate for this age group. If your room, routines, and pedagogy are set up to foster children's autonomy (see the Red, Orange, and Yellow chapters), your students are not sitting in individual desks, in straight rows, silently completing worksheets. They are a constant blur of sound and motion: talking, asking questions, moving through the room to find materials. This can be disconcerting and at times, exhausting, but here's the thing: they are not doing anything wrong.

For many of us, our adult brains crave order and quiet. When we look at a group of young children with our adult eyes, connected to our adult brain, their chatter and movement seem alarming. "This is chaos!" our brains scream, and our impulse is to extinguish the chaos. We set rigid schedules, create highly specific expectations, develop rituals to keep everyone in lockstep. The problem is: these things are not for them. They are for you (or, in some settings, they are for your administrators – and that will require a whole other level of management. We will get to that, too.)

Setting the Stage: Agreeing on Rules

Co-creating the classroom "rules" is not a new concept. Basically, as part of your first day of school, you work with your students to brainstorm the rules for your classroom for the year. Most often, you write these rules on a poster that then hangs in your room. Often, there is a step where every student signs the poster, with their name or their handprint.

While our tone here may be flippant, this is a good and useful activity. We like it! We have done it ourselves! We encourage you to do the same! There are, however, a few small tweaks that will make this activity more appropriate, meaningful, and useful to both you and your students.

First: the word "rules" carries a certain negative weight, and there are many ways to reframe this process more positively. Some examples:

- *Code of cooperation*
- *Mission statement*
- *Class contract*
- *Class charter*
- *Class agreement*
- *We promise…*
- *Our values*

Here's the big key: whatever this document/poster is called, it should have no more than three rules. That's right. Three. Why only three? Because most five-year-olds can memorize three things very quickly, and if you want your students to live by these rules, they need to know them by heart.

These three rules need to cover EVERYTHING. Any possible problem/concern/issue/scenario needs to be able to fall under the umbrella of at least one of them. This means they need to be broad and flexible. At the same time, these rules must use words that are clear and meaningful to young learners. If you find yourself including words that may be unclear to some of your students, either simplify the words or work in a vocabulary lesson.

Here's an example from early in Amy's career:

In a first-grade classroom, on the first day of school, we sat down on the carpet, and I asked the question: "What are some things we can agree on that will help us have a good year together?"

Because they were six-year-olds, the conversation started with things like "No throwing things at other people"; "Don't say bad words like the s-word"; "No licking the floor or your chair"; "No hiding in the coatroom to eat candy."

I pointed out that these were are all things that we would NOT do, and gently suggested we come up with some things that we WOULD do. This led us to: "When someone is hurt, tell a teacher"; "Say please"; "Say sorry if you do something bad"; "If someone is crying, give them a hug."

I wrote all of their suggestions on the board. ALL of them. Yes, including "No licking the floor or your chair."

When the initial gush of suggestions started to slow down, I paused, looked at the board, and pointed out the themes that I saw there: "I notice that many of our ideas are about being kind." We circled all the things related to kindness. We did the same for politeness, and for honesty. We then double-checked to make sure each of our ideas fit into one of these three categories.

We then ended up with a poster that said:

In this classroom:
We are kind.
We are polite.
We are honest.

We talked about those three words – kind, polite, honest – all year. The words provided a framework when students called one another out (and also when they tattled!). Parents reported that these three words became a chorus in their homes, as well.

TABLE 5.1

Co-creating the rules, an example from Amy's classroom

We are kind.	*We are polite.*	*We are honest.*
No throwing things at other people.	Don't say bad words like the s-word.	No hiding in the coatroom to eat candy.
When someone is hurt, tell a teacher.	No licking the floor or your chair.	Say sorry if you do something bad.
If someone is crying, give them a hug.	Say please.	Don't pretend that something imaginary is true.

Having three broad-but-clear, easy-to-remember rules/agreements/values gives you a road map to follow for the entire year. You will not need to come up with new rules for field trips or classroom guests or your weekly library period. No matter where you go, or what you do, your students are kind/polite/honest/respectful/brave/determined, and so on. With this framework, all you need for each new event or experience is a class discussion of "what does kind/polite/honest look like: in the library/when we have a guest/on a nature walk/etc.?"

These words will help create community and a healthy classroom culture. As the teacher, these words apply to you, too. They apply to anyone who comes into your room. When a new student joins you, these words are among the first things they learn about their new classroom.

Taming the Chaos

In the Red chapter, we talked about explicitly teaching classroom routines, and not assuming that your students know how to:

- line up.
- move between areas of the room.
- organize and use materials.
- clean up after themselves.

Intentionally and systematically teaching, modeling, and practicing these things will save you mountains of time and frustration throughout the year, and reduce the need for behavioral support for individual students. When children know what to do, and how to do it, they are calmer, quieter. and more regulated.

Creating Independent Problem-Solvers (So YOU Don't Have to Referee!)

Most kindergarten social conflicts can be boiled down to "my classmate is doing something I don't like." Equipping students to navigate these situations on their own is surprisingly easy, and will free up hours of your time and energy.

It is empowering for young children to advocate for themselves, and to know that their voice will be respected. We recommend the following steps for "when someone is doing something you do not like":

1. Tell the other person to stop, using a clear voice: "Please stop that, I don't like it." (Practice saying this exact phrase, out loud, clearly. Kids can also hold up one hand in front of them, in a "stop" gesture). If the person stops, great! Problem solved! If they do not stop, move to step 2.
2. Say it again, louder. (It's important for children to know that it is OK to yell if they need to; yelling is preferable to hitting or pushing.) If the person stops, great! Problem solved! If they do not stop, move to step 3.
3. Get help from an adult. Tell the adult what happened, that you said stop, and that the other person did not stop.

There are two critical pieces to making this procedure work:

1. Enforcing that **"stop" means <u>stop</u>**. This is a powerful message for young children to internalize; it is the beginning of teaching consent, which is an important lifelong lesson.
2. Ensuring that, once a child gets to step 3, an adult **will** help. A child who has followed the steps and is now seeking adult support cannot be dismissed as "tattling." Now that they need help, **we must provide it**. This means you will need to enlist the support of anyone else who interacts with your students: specialist teachers, educational assistants, recess or lunchroom supervisors, librarians, parent volunteers, and so on. **Everyone** needs to know that if one of your students approaches them, asking for help, it is because they have already tried to solve the problem themselves.

If you can get your entire school on board with learning and following this procedure, it is incredibly powerful. When a child knows that every other student understands stop means stop, and that they can reliably get help from any adult, any time, it creates a strong community of empowered children.

When they get to step 3:
Often, when a child approaches you because they have reached step 3, all they will need is an adult (you!) to support them while they repeat their request for the classmate to stop the bothersome behavior. As your classroom culture grows, and students know that you are serious about "stop means stop," they will need less and less help to resolve these issues.

The Role of the Peacemaker and the Problem-Solving Center

As we discussed in the Green chapter on facilitating play and room design, doing a little front work to get your peacemaking center operational will help solidify a class culture of independent problem-solvers. As conflicts arise, help children move to dialogue chairs and help them take turns explaining the issue. This can get quite hot sometimes, and calming down may take a moment if they are crying. "Sofia, look how much Petunia is crying, she is really upset. Can we give her a few minutes to calm down before we talk together?" This gets Petunia thinking and *she* may start crying as well. Teacher: "Wow, I can see you both feel really bad about what happened. Can we work together to fix it now?"

When Things Get More Serious

There are, of course, specific behaviors that will need your intervention and investigation, and probably some parent communication. The most common of these will involve an outburst of physical aggression. When little Elliott comes to you, wailing that "Georgia hit me!" you'll need to gather some information before you issue consequences for Georgia. And sometimes, this investigation is the hardest thing you do in a day.

Here's the thing: as we talked about in the Yellow chapter on child development, kindergarten-aged students are more than capable of outright lying and lying by omission. Even if Elliot is telling the truth about Georgia hitting him, he may have left out the fact that he was pulling Georgia's hair and she had asked him three times to stop. Often, you can put the pieces together pretty easily, but sometimes (especially if some time has gone by, like if students are reporting something that happened at recess and you were not outside), it can seem impossible to get a clear story. Here are some tips that may help:

- Ask what was going on immediately before the problem occurred: "What was going on right before she hit you?"
- Use a gentle, calm, neutral tone to encourage truth-telling.
- If the incident occurred when you were not present, ask if another adult has already helped solve this problem, or if there was an adult nearby who may have seen what happened. (If the PE teacher or recess supervisor has already been involved, you can follow up with them later.)
- Ask if there was another student who was involved or may have seen what happened.
- Wait until all involved students are calm before you start investigating. "I can see we need to figure out what happened, but we all need to be calm, first. Would you like to sit in the peacekeeping center and take some deep breaths?"

Young children do not have strong chronological storytelling skills, and will often start their story with the part that is more important to them, not necessarily the part that occurred first chronologically. When you are ready to start investigating, start with Elliot and have him tell you everything, **while you write it down**. Read it back to him and let him correct anything that is not in order. Before moving on to Georgia, ask Elliott: "When I read this to Georgia, will she agree that this is what happened?" Move on to Georgia, read Elliott's account, and make any additions/changes. Move on to any other children who were involved or who saw what happened. While this will take a little time, it will help you get a relatively clear picture of what happened, to whom, and why.

Making Amends

Five-year-olds are pretty self-centered, and their level of sincere empathy can be inconsistent. While it is a good and honorable impulse to want a student to apologize when they have hurt or upset someone, it may not be realistic to expect that apology to be really deeply felt by the child who is producing it. Some kindergarten students do feel true remorse when they have hurt a classmate, but for many, their remorse is for themselves because they are "in trouble." Additionally, many have come to see apologies as a "get out of jail free" card that will erase the offense. It's OK to value and practice apologies as a social courtesy, even before a child truly feels sorry, but we like to accompany the apology with an act of reparation. The key lessons here is that **when we hurt or bother someone, even by accident, we apologize and try to make things better.**

Here is one possible script that can help a child formulate a clear and complete apology and offer of amends: *"I'm sorry that I _______. I know it made you feel _____. What can I do to make it better?"*

> *Example: "I'm sorry that I pushed you. I know it made you feel sad. What can I do to make it better?"*

You will be surprised at the richness of students' ideas for what can make it better. Responses we have heard include the following:

- Give me a hug.
- Hold my hand until I feel better.
- Clean up the mess (when a box of crayons was knocked to the floor).
- Leave me alone for a while.
- Just let me be mad until I feel not mad anymore.
- Tell me a joke.
- Don't do it again
- Use nicer words next time.

- Play with me at recess.
- Get me an ice pack.
- Go play somewhere else for a while.
- Don't do this to anyone else ever again.

And yes, there will always be students who try to work this to their own advantage when they are the victim, by claiming the only thing that will "make it better" is for the "aggressor" to share their dessert, or hand over a treasured toy. These demands are, of course, inappropriate (even if they are amusing), and can be avoided by a class brainstorming session of "ways to make it better."

Defining and Understanding a "Problem" Behavior

What about the behaviors that go beyond "my classmate is doing something I do not like?" The ones that really get under your skin, and that are bothering other students? Don't those behaviors need more specific, targeted solutions?

First: be patient. Unless a behavior is a legitimate threat to the safety of others (yourself included), give it at least four to six weeks into the school year before you address it in a targeted and specific way. Some children will display unexpected behaviors as part of settling into a new environment or adapting to new routines. The first several weeks of "real school" are tremendously exciting, and excitement is a form of stress. None of us are at our best under stress. Work on routines, be consistent, use the vocabulary in your class agreement, and see if things improve.

OK, so you have made your classroom contract, your students understand the vocabulary, and you are all building the habit of embedding it into your classroom culture. You have practiced routines and been patient as students learn how to "do school." You have taught your students the script for when something is bothering them, most of them are using it, and "stop means stop" is starting to be effective. What now? What to do about the behaviors that are persistent, bothersome, and seem to be immune to everything you have done so far?

Defining the Behavior

Once you are past the settling in period, you will almost certainly start to identify some behaviors that feel like problems. Here is the framework Amy uses when talking a teacher through a student's behavior:

1. *What specifically is the student doing that is a problem?*
   If you can't specifically describe exactly what the student is doing, you are not going to be able to support them in changing it. The answer to this first question needs to be specific, observable things a child does, not your interpretation of their thoughts, feelings, or motivations. (We will get to motivation in a short while. It does matter, but not just yet.)

2. *Why is this a problem?*
   Here is where we get to a hard truth: a behavior that is annoying to you is not necessarily a problem that needs fixing. It is so easy to forget this when a child is grating on your nerves, but sometimes the easiest "solution" is for you to reframe it, ignore it, or let it go.
   A child's behavior is a problem if (and only if) it:

   - compromises their own safety, or the safety of other members of the school community.
   - disrupts their own learning or the learning of others.

   Note that "safety" and "learning" are both multidimensional constructs. If a child's annoying behavior is preventing them from having positive peer relationships, it is compromising their own emotional safety and their social-emotional learning.

3. *When and where does this behavior occur?*
   Record each time the behavior occurs, using the table below and the following definitions for each column. Keep recording until you have 10 to 12 specific occurrences. Depending on the child and the particular behavior, this may take you a whole week, or just a day or so.

TABLE 5.2

Behavior data tracking table

Date & time	*What?*	*Where?*	*Who?*

- What?
  What was going on at the time the behavior occurred? What activity, routine, or transition?
- Where?
  Where in the classroom or school did it occur? Be specific: if it was on the playground, was it near the swings or the slide?
- Who?
  - Which other children were involved or nearby? Who was the target of the behavior? Who was the child playing with? Was a staff member involved or interacting with this student at the time?

4. *What need is this behavior meeting?*

This is where you get to think about the child's motivation. Behavior is communication, and if a child is doing something, there is always a reason. To help resolve the behavior, we need to play detective and figure out the reason. Using the data you collected in step 3, consider the following:

- **Basic physical needs:** What do you know about this child's sleep routine? Their diet? Water intake? Even the most self-possessed adult can be irritable when tired, hungry, or thirsty, and this is even truer for young children. If your data shows that a child is often lashing out at others just before snack time, is it possible to adjust the timing of the snack? Can you allow students to eat when they are hungry rather than scheduling whole-group snack time? If a student is distractible and inattentive on Monday mornings, can you speak with a parent about their Sunday bedtime routine?

- **Developmental needs:** As we discussed in the Yellow chapter, little bodies are constantly growing, and the best way for a child to understand their continuously changing body is to seek stimulation and test their own limits. Behaviors such as fidgeting, wiggling, and bumping into things or people can often be related to this. Consider whether the behavior is helping a child do any of these:
  - seek or avoid sensory input
  - adjust muscle or joint positioning
  - understand their own shape, size, strength, and balance
- **Social-emotional needs:** A child's behavior is often an attempt to communicate an emotion, fill a gap in their social skills, or meet a critical social-emotional need. Picture the behavior in your mind, and consider whether they may be seeking any of the following:
  - attention
  - connection
  - affection
  - control
  - release for a strong emotion (anger, sadness)
  - self-protection
  - relief from fear or anxiety

A note about vision: poor vision can affect a child's progress and development in ways that go far beyond academics. A child who cannot see well may constantly be in other children's personal space in an effort to see their classmates' features better, or because they are less aware of where their own body is in space. Similarly, they may seek sensory input through touch by fidgeting with and even breaking classroom materials. All children should have a thorough eye exam before starting school. We recommend asking parents about eye exams at your first "meet the teacher" or classroom open house event, and following up throughout the year. Your principal, district, or school nurse may be able to share resources for affordable children's eye care in your area.

Doing Something About "Problem" Behavior: Supporting the Child

When You Have Identified the Need

The behavior is meeting a need. How can that need be met in a more appropriate way? Sometimes, it is up to you, as the adult, to ensure that the need is met so that the child does not have to rely on the problematic behavior. This is most challenging when a behavior is for the purpose of seeking affection, attention, and connection. When a child is behaving in an annoying, unacceptable, or even dangerous way, to get your attention, it can be easy to fall into the trap of believing the child is being manipulative and/or malicious, and to then decide that withdrawing your attention or affection even further is the appropriate response. STOP THINKING LIKE THAT, RIGHT NOW.

If we know a child gets aggressive when they are hungry, we would ensure that they eat regularly. We would not withhold food until they behave. We would keep that little tummy full of healthy calories and nutrients. If we look at connection/attention/affection the same way as food or water, we need to provide it **before** the problematic behavior emerges.

Ways to proactively fill the need for attention/connection/affection:

- Greet the child individually and enthusiastically, by name, as they arrive in class. Make eye contact and smile at them as you do so, as if you have been eagerly waiting for them to arrive.

- Ensure the child gets a turn to speak during your morning circle/meeting time, preferably at the first opportunity.
- If possible, have the child arrive a few minutes early and come in to help you set up the classroom for the day, or stay a few minutes late to help you tidy up (this is only effective if the child experiences this as a treat rather than a punishment).
- As part of your arrival routine, take a moment to quietly check in, individually, with that child: comment on what they are doing, ask questions, connect.
- Use gentle, appropriate physical contact to establish connection: a hand on their shoulder or back as you walk by, letting them hold your hand as you move through the room or building, high fives, handshakes, fist bumps.
- Let them help with a special task or run an errand to the office or supply room.
- Remember details of upcoming events or milestones, and ask the child about them: "How was dinner at grandma's?" "Tell me about your soccer game!"
- During free play, join in their activity, or invite them to play a board or card game with you.

If you have identified that the source of a behavior is a need for connection, spend two weeks focusing on your relationship and connection with that child, and ignoring the behavior as much as possible. You may find that the behavior resolves itself, because the underlying need is being met.

Real Talk: When YOU Are the One Struggling with Connection

While we may be reluctant to admit it, every teacher, at some point in their career, will encounter a child who is hard to like. This is a normal part of being human and not a personal failure! Just as you sometimes encounter adults who rub you the wrong way, you will meet children who frustrate, aggravate, irritate, and annoy you. The important thing is to recognize this feeling so that your own behavior does not reflect it. You can use the same strategies described above to ensure you are providing that child with a sense of connection (and hopefully, being intentional about your relationship will help you develop an authentic affection for that child while you are at it!). Every child deserves to feel like their teacher likes them.

When You Have Identified the Trigger

Sometimes, the need may not be clear, but your data does show a pattern for when/where the behavior occurs. Now that you have the data, it is your professional responsibility to use it to help this child. If you have done the work of finding patterns in Isaac's behavior, and you know that Isaac lashes out in anger every time he loses a soccer game in PE class, you need a plan for when he loses his next soccer game. If Diana melts down every time she is not first in line, you need a plan for every time Diana gets in line.

Let's say that Olivia pushes other students every time the coatroom gets crowded. How can you change that context, to eliminate the trigger?

Option 1: Change the routine for everyone. It is perfectly OK to change the whole class' routine as a way to support one child's struggle with unsafe behavior. Often, this carries advantages for all the children. Teaching the whole class to gather their winter clothing from their cubbies and then move into the main classroom area to find a personal space to get dressed will not only take Olivia out of a situation that was difficult for her, but it will take all the students out of a setting that was highly stimulating and therefore rich with opportunities for conflict and high emotion. (Of course, you are not going to TELL everyone that you are changing this routine for Olivia! You are going to tell them that you are changing the routine to make it work better for everyone.) Olivia's dignity is protected, and everyone is safer, calmer.

Option 2: Change the routine for Olivia. If changing the environment for everyone is not an option, can you change the environment for Olivia in a way that respects her dignity and helps her feel supported? The same change can feel like a gift or a punishment, depending on how it is presented. For example: if you decide to change the location of Olivia's cubby, you could announce: "Olivia, you have to stop pushing in the coatroom, so I am moving your cubby where I can keep an eye on you."

This will likely extinguish the pushing, but it will also probably embarrass Olivia, and stigmatize both her and her new cubby.

BUT: you could also take Olivia aside, quietly, and say: "It seems like the coatroom is a hard place for you, and you have trouble managing your feelings when it's crowded. I'm wondering if it would help if we found a new spot for your cubby. Maybe somewhere near the door? Where I could help you if I saw that you were getting overwhelmed? Let's go look together and see if we can find a better spot."

Imagine the relief for Olivia when she knows that her teacher sees that this is hard for her, and has a plan to help her.

Most of the time, the careful work of observing and documenting will give you the data you need to reduce the problematic behavior, or at least to soften its impact.

Thoughts on Behavior Charts

You'll note that we are three-fourths of the way through a chapter on classroom management and behavior, and we have not yet discussed behavior charts. This is not a mistake. As a general rule, we do not recommend or support the use of behavior charts. These systems (whether on paper or digital, whether they involve moving a clip or flipping a card) amount to public shaming, creating stigma for students who need support the most. Children need relationships, not systems, to help them express their needs in safe and appropriate ways. We could (and maybe someday will) write an entire book about how and why to run your classroom without these tools.

When You MUST Have a Behavior Chart Because Your District Says So … How to Make It Work

We also know that some schools and districts mandate the use of some kind of behavior chart or reward system in every classroom. If that is your situation, this section is for you!

If you must have a behavior chart or reward system:

- Make it private and discreet. Can each child keep a personal chart in their basket or cubby, or in a binder that only you and they can see? When you provide feedback, do so quietly, not in front of the class.

- Make it individualized. Let each child set a goal for the day or week. Praise and reward progress rather than hold the whole class to the same standard of perfection.
- Focus on self-reflection and support. If you are required to have a publicly posted chart, let students decide for themselves when they need to move their clip or flip their card. Frame a moved clip as a request for support rather than a failure.
- Reward with experiences, not trinkets. If your system must include rewards, do so without using a treasure box. Reward with non-tangible experiences such as getting to eat lunch at the teacher's desk, or choosing the book at story time.

Managing Your Own Behavior

Helping all these small people manage their own behavior and impulses is exhausting and emotional work. It will stretch your patience to the breaking point. What to do when you're feeling out of control and completely frustrated?

First: don't beat yourself up. We have all been there. Then:

- Go outside, with the children if you have to. Fresh air will be good for all of you. Even a quick five-minute walk around the perimeter of the playground will help clear your head and reset your emotions.
- Read a story. Call everyone to the carpet, and read a favorite classroom story, one that you all know and love, that keeps the children engaged, and that you can read on autopilot.
- Sing songs. Loudly, and with actions.
- Color. Pull out some coloring sheets (we especially like abstract or mandala designs because they encourage sequencing/patterning skills), put on some quiet music, and have everybody (you included) color for five or ten minutes.

- Watch a video. Yes, we said it. Keep a few DVDs or YouTube links tucked away, of short, kid-friendly video content. Many children's authors have YouTube channels that feature digital storybook versions of their work.
- Call for backup. Who in your building can you call, to keep an eye on your class while you step out and breathe for three minutes? Can the teacher next door stand between your two rooms, doors open, and keep an eye on things? Will the secretary pop down to your room for a few minutes?
- Fill your water bottle and take three deep breaths while the water runs.
- Sneak a piece of chocolate and chew it slowly.
- Wash your hands, very slowly and thoroughly. Warm water is relaxing, but cold water can also have a useful grounding effect!
- If you do not have a sink in the room (or even if you do), rub lotion into your hands. It's like a tiny little hand massage!

Managing your classroom, and helping students who need support with their behavior is often the most demanding and time-consuming thing you do. It is also perhaps the most important, and most rewarding part of working with young children.

Assessment Checklist: When a Behavior May Need More Expertise Than Yours Alone

Inevitably, you will, at some point, encounter a child whose needs truly do exceed the capacities of a single classroom teacher. The list below will give you an idea of when to ask for help from your principal, resource teacher, school psychologist, or other supports:

- This child is physically aggressive with other children most days, multiple times per day.
- This child is physically aggressive with adults.

- This child regularly makes violent threats against other children and/or adults ("I'm going to kill you." "My daddy has a gun and I will shoot you." "I will cut you into pieces.")
- This child has emotional outbursts that are more intense, sustained, or frequent than their peers.
- This child has emotional outbursts that are disruptive to their own learning.
- This child has (or has attempted to) run away from the group/playground/classroom on multiple occasions.
- This child puts other children at risk by throwing toys, pushing furniture, and so forth.
- This child is defiant (deliberately does not follow instructions or requests) more often than they are compliant.
- You have received multiple complaints/questions/concerns from other parents about this child.
- Other children are fearful of this child.
- Specialist teachers have expressed concerns about this child's behavior in their programs.
- This child requires one-on-one behavioral support and intervention for many/most classroom activities.
- This child requires significantly more attention/supervision than most other children in the class.

References and Recommended Reading

Carrington, J. (2020). *Kids these days: A game plan for (re)connecting with those we teach, lead, & love.* Impress.

Copple, C., & Bredekamp, S. (Eds.). (2008). *Developmentally appropriate practice in early childhood programs serving children from birth through age 8* (3d ed.). National Association for the Education of Young Children (NAEYC).

Erdman, S., Colker, L. J., & Winter, E. C., (2020). *Trauma and young children: Teaching strategies to support and empower.* National Association for the Education of Young Children (NAEYC).

Ripp, P. (2014.) *Before you hang up that public behavior chart.* https://pernillesripp.com/2014/11/29/before-you-hang-up-that-public-behavior-chart/

Ripp, P. (2016.) *I've had enough – no more public behavior management systems.* https://pernillesripp.com/2016/06/28/ive-had-enough-no-more-public-behavior-management-systems/

Smith, D., Fisher, D., & Frey, N. (2015). *Better than carrots or sticks: Restorative practices for positive classroom management.* Association for Supervision & Curriculum Development

6

Indigo: Research, Readings, Assessing, and Documenting Learning

The classroom is running, you are teaching curriculum, and you are finally starting to feel like the actual ringmaster rather than the clown running around with a fire hose… Then your principal comes in talking about writing a grant to teach reading using electroshock aversion therapy. He read about it on Facebook, so it must be true! How do you stay on top of new research, without getting caught up in every new trend and acronym? How do you become your students' strongest, most knowledgeable advocate, without drowning in mountains of professional reading every night?

Basic Philosophies

Let's start by becoming familiar with a few foundational practices and philosophies. While there are many philosophies out there, two major ones every educator should know are Montessori and Reggio Emilia. There are multiple differences, but generally, one is more skills based and the other is more process based.

TABLE 6.1

Comparison of Montessori and Reggio philosophies

Montessori: Maria Montessori (1906)	*Reggio Emilia: Loris Malaguzzi (1972)*
Emphasis on progression of skills	Emphasis on constructivism and documentation
Self-correcting materials designed to teach specific skills and concepts	Emphasis on the process of learning through the Project Approach
Focus on individual child achievement; children grouped multi-age	Focus on child's role within a society and the collective responsibility of the community
Mussolini demands Montessori programs pledge alliance; Montessori schools close in Italy after Maria Montessori refuses	Reggio philosophy developed in reaction to Mussolini's fascism
Role of teacher is observer and preparer of environment	Role of teacher is researcher and interpreter
Practical life centers incorporated, emphasis on independence	Art and the atelier central to the learning environment
Beautiful materials	Beautiful materials
Philosophy extends past early childhood	Philosophy extends past early childhood

Which Philosophy Do I Choose?

For most educators, it's not an either-or choice. To fully "do" each of these philosophies, you need specialized training. Comparing Reggio and Montessori is really a "skills" based approach versus a "process" approach, and the study and knowledge of each represents the constant back-and-forth swing of educational philosophy. Each and every philosophy out there has merits and drawbacks. There's not one "perfect" practice. Our job as teachers is being aware and informed that there are wide varieties of approaches to educating children. You learn to take a bit from here and from there to help you tailor your own program to your needs. Whatever the case, learning from and studying these and other educational philosophies is essential ongoing study to help you grow your practice.

How and Why to Stay Current

As a teacher, you are never "done" learning. Your entire career should be one of constant learning and revising. Finding new inspiration for learning can come from anywhere. Keep your eyes open and follow what interests you and the children you observe. Inspiration can come from attending professional conferences, from talking with colleagues in person or through networks like #Kinderchat, and from reading articles, books, and new research. We have provided a library of resources for you to look through at kinderchat.org.

The Difficulty of Accessing Research

One of the most challenging aspects of classroom teaching is the work of accessing and disseminating real, actual research related to the field of learning and teaching. It often feels as if there is a great divide between those studying the learning processes of children and those doing the day-in and day-out work of teaching and learning with children. Most research is held behind university access and can often be so academic in scope that it can be hard to disseminate or find relevance when you are desperately looking for an article to help you figure out why Shawna keeps doing that thing with her mouth, or what additional structures and supports you can put in to help find her name consistently.

Sometimes all you really want is an article telling José's parents that before he reads *War and Peace* next week, he first needs to learn to dress himself each morning and needs more practice clapping along with the music, because music is directly related to reading, but good luck finding that article. Instead, you will find articles on how wind instrument training had a moderate effect on preservice teachers in Turkey teaching reading. If you do manage to sift through and find a few articles on the correlation between music and early reading, you can often get "a small number of studies show"-type of language, which you know is not going to convince José's parents.

Meanwhile, you *know* that Jose cannot keep a beat and there is a direct reflection on his ability to do that and learn to read. You know that having him do more music and rhythm work will help him with his phonemic skills, and that he needs to do *even more,* not half as much, instead of being skilled and drilled on sight words and little games to help him decipher lowercase n's.

Alternatively, you can get swamped in research on homework or the famous phonics fight with six articles on either side and language so subtle and specific that you soon lose track of what they're even talking about. Reaching back to your college stats class to interpret graph number 67 gets tricky when your mind is continually focused on 16 things you can do with a cardboard box, and, oh please, can Cindy Lou JUST SIT DOWN FOR FIVE SECONDS TODAY? Revisiting those skills is a valuable exercise. Don't get us wrong. We are just saying practitioners can get just as squirmy and avoidant as any kid on the rug for too long.

Teachers, acting as translators for children and their behavior and development, also need translators of academic integrity to help us apply research to our daily work.

How to Tell Good Info from Bad

Enter the edu-expert. There's a reason these folks are out there! There are experts in just about every aspect of edu-data and best practices, and you need them. When you are in the everyday here and now, these folks help lift you up and bring moments of clarity (or add in some new confusion – learning is messy!) as you work to untangle information and make sense of it all to apply it to your classroom.

We get that many teachers insist upon practical "take-back" strategies they can immediately implement in the classroom, but we urge as much insistence upon professional development that is informed by research and active pedagogical practice. Your ultimate job as an educator is not "16 new ways to teach phonics," but rather, to be constantly learning about learning.

The world of social media has opened up avenues of access to information both good and bad. While there are a million subtleties, our overall yardstick is to listen to people who share the complexity of the story. Whether that be data or best practices, there is impressive complexity to the educational system. It's often difficult to untangle and make sense of, and it takes work. Learning is never finite. To start, find reliable, well-known and respected edu-leaders and spend a lot of time listening, engaging, and reading.

Navigating Social Media as a Professional Resource

Many of you reading this may have been born into a world already fluent in social media, but for us old-timers over 40, there was certainly a learning curve as social media became the norm, and even more so when it became a professional and public learning tool for teachers.

> *When Amy and I first found each other on Twitter back in 2008, it was literally all business people. We 'met' because we were early childhood educators. That soon led to us finding even more early childhood folks on Twitter and so was born #Kinderchat.*
>
> *Heidi*

Now you can find any number of communities of early childhood folks out there on just about every platform there is, though we have a clear preference for Twitter. Social media is constantly changing and highly dynamic, so it can be frustrating to learn and keep up with, but it also can provide some of the most effective and rewarding FREE professional development out there. Many folks in the education sphere tweet regularly. We suggest @ garystager and @alfiekohn to get you started. Gary Stager, PhD, is an expert on constructivism and computing, and hosts professional development opportunities and features extensive listings of resources on his blog and website. Alfie Kohn is a prolific writer on education, behavior, children, schools, and parenting. See who they follow, reference, and read. There are also TONS of college and university professors on Twitter on every subject from climate change to history to educational practices. Find them, follow, and learn.

Exchanging information and tips with colleagues from around the world helps you gain perspective on your own little corner of the world. Through social media, you can become friends with talented early educators from around the globe; there are opportunities for ongoing interaction that a conference or one-time event could have never provided. Be sure to at least follow a few online groups or conversations as part of your ongoing professional development.

A Word of Caution about Edu-celebrities

When Twitter chats were really taking off, so was born the educeleb, the instant Internet influencer. While following this type of influencer can be a helpful tool, it's more important that you EXCHANGE information with colleagues and read articles based on research and best practices instead of consuming prescheduled tweets offering an endless stream of "5 tips for teachers" clickbait.

Sharing Learning

Methods of Providing Evidence of Learning

Whether it be your own or your students', sharing learning is an important part of the process of learning. One of the most wonderful things about teaching early readers and writers is that they are more difficult to "test" in the conventional sense. This helps create space for educators to expand on the idea of demonstrating learning through more unconventional means. Ideally, you use and incorporate each of these methods into your practice to help provide evidence of each child's learning.

- Observation and Reflections
- Dialogue
  - Interviews and ongoing dialogue with individual students
  - Ongoing dialogue with the class as a whole
- Documentation
  - Children's art, drawings, and writing samples
  - Photographs and videos

- Formal assessments and skill checklists
- Student presentations of work to community (school, parents, town)
- Written Teacher Feedback and Reflections
  - To students
  - To parents

Project/Unit Launch	Work Time	Wrap Up
Observation and Reflections **Dialogue** Interviews and ongoing dialogue with individual student Ongoing dialogue with the class as a whole	**Documentation and Sharing of Learning** Collect art, drawings and writing samples Photographs and video documentation Student presentations of work to community Formal assessments and/or skill checklists	**Written Feedback/ Reflections** To students To families

FIGURE 6.1
Project time line

Observation and Reflections

Your observations and reflections are the most powerful assessment tool available to you. Spend twice as much time quietly observing your class at work as you do teaching lessons, especially at first. Watching children at work and play will inform your practice, telling you where you need to go next as well as helping you learn the strengths and challenges each child faces in their school life. Teachers should be constantly working to translate child developmental continuums into visible examples of authentic children's work and ongoing communication between parent, child, and community.

What a Good Cut-and-Paste Project Teaches You about Children's Skills

One of the best assessments you can do is a good old-fashioned cut-and-paste project. Observing how children approach this basic skill teaches you VOLUMES about their approach to learning, their persistence, and their problem-solving skills, all while letting you assess visual-motor tracking, planning, and fine motor skills.

A good place to start is with a self-portrait. Starting with a self-portrait opens up discussions on identity and the diversity of humans.

Materials:

- Read-aloud talking about and celebrating the many hair, skin, and eye colors that humans come in
- Skin-tone construction paper representative of multiple hair and skin colors
- Multicolored construction papers
- Scissors, glue
- Paper to work on

The key to a good cut-and-paste project is to NOT GIVE THEM a template, stencil, or line to follow. Following a line while cutting is a different skill you can tuck into the writing center or do during a math lesson on shapes. For this particular project, you are asking the kids to VISUALIZE and hold in their mind what a shape looks like to represent their head, body, arms, and legs, and then to cut that shape out. Already there's a lot going on: they have to visualize the shape, keep that shape in their head, and then actually cut it out. You'll always have a few who want to trace or draw a line, but encourage them to try it without those guidelines. ***PLEASE KNOW YOU ARE NOT ASSESSING THEIR ABILITY TO CUT OUT A PERFECT CIRCLE.*** You are OBSERVING their approach to the task, their perception, and their placement of objects. Some assessment questions you might think about:

- Are they frequently fighting over scissors, glue, paper, and space with the person next to them, or do they work cooperatively in groups?
- Are they spread out over a gigantic space or working within a defined space?
- Do they lose track of what they are doing?
- Have they used glue before? Are they comfortable using their fingers for gluing? Worried about touching the glue?

- How long did they take to complete the project? Did they stay on task?
- How much detail did they add to their portrait?
- Were they engaged with the project?
- Were they frustrated at any time? What frustrated them and why?
- Did they clean their work space up? Did they plan out all the different colored papers they needed, or go back to the well each time?
- Did they use a variety of papers or just a few colors?
- How was their scissor grip?

Ideally, you'll do multiple cutting projects throughout your program all year. Save their portrait from the beginning of the year, and then you can have them do another at the end of the year to compare the growth. You will be amazed! Use these portraits as the front and back covers of their writing portfolio to show evidence of growth!

Interviews and Dialogue

Writing down class discussions as dialogue is a powerful way we can learn from constructivist educational philosophy. In 2016, schools in Ontario, Canada, adopted inquiry- and play-based kindergarten programs and incorporated methods of documenting learning and sharing learning. A wonderful, accessible example of this is from Aviva Dunsiger (@avivaloca on Twitter). Be sure to check out her class blog and website for her impressive examples of ongoing classroom documentation. What does the following conversation teach you about children's thinking? Why is it important to document this thinking? Why might sharing this conversation with parents and the greater community be a benefit? Below is an example of a conversation you might have with your class:

> *We were out playing and noticed the leaves were all over the ground! And they were different colors! Ms. Echternacht couldn't believe someone would tear all the leaves off the trees and paint them like that. What's happened out there?!*

Someone said, "No, that's supposed to happen! It's fall. That's what happens in the fall."

Teacher: "But why?! Why now? Why do they fall off?! How is that even possible to change colors? Are trees magic?"

"No! No one painted them! They just change."

"The wind blows and it makes the colors change."

"No! That doesn't make sense because it was windy in the summertime too."

"The colder it gets, the heavier the leaves get and they fall down."

"The leaves are happy."

"They change on the first day of fall."

"Maybe it has to do with water."

"They don't fall! They connect down. When it's not fall, they connect up."

'They are hanging there and they just can't take it anymore and they fall off!"

Then someone noticed that the brown leaves were crinkly and fell apart easily, and the green ones were harder to tear. We will continue digging into this science question!

Interviews with Individual Students

Many programs focus on individual time spent with students. While we find this valuable, we also find that young children can be skittish with adults – even you, their teacher. Some children demand your time, others completely avoid you, and still others float in and out of your radar – and that may change throughout the year! Sometimes it can be awkward having a scheduled 1:1 conversation with a young child, even for experienced teachers.

Marcus really wants to get back to playing rather than spend time talking with you about 5 + 2 = 7 and 2 + 5 = 7. As soon as you called him over for a meeting, José took his truck. While he's distracted and keeping an eye on José, he will still sit with you and talk about this completely uninteresting thing called math because he likes you and Marcus wants to be good. He will deal with the truck issue later, which may involve punching José for taking it in the first place or resolving it in a more peaceful manner, all depending.

Despite all of the obstacles and complications, 1:1 time is absolutely a valuable opportunity for feedback. Whether it be a formal interview where you record the child's answers, or you just spend time talking about their latest project, be sure you are regularly checking in with each student, even if for just a few minutes on the playground every day.

Documenting the Process of Learning

Authentic Children's Work

Very often people aren't aware of what actual children's work even looks like. The worst offender of "authentic children's work" can generally be found on bulletin boards. Frequently, most of the "work" we see around classrooms is "artwork" where the child simply paints a few circles or egg cartons green, and the teacher "helps" assemble it into a caterpillar, plant, or leprechaun. Meanwhile, the child has absolutely no idea why he is filling previously cut-out construction paper fruits into a cornucopia. Well-intentioned teachers will often try to control the work of children and twist it into carbon copy "cute" projects that are actually adult ideas of what *they think* children's work should look like, rather than what it actually looks like. Too often, children's authentic work is invisible, unappreciated, or dismissed as irrelevant.

Authentic student work is completely driven by the student. The teacher is there to guide, question, and help form the habits of mind and culture that take the child to the next question and proposed solution. Give children the gift of space to allow them to figure out solutions for themselves. Can you recognize where students are? Can you discern REAL authentic children's work? What questions might you ask these students to help guide their projects forward?

> *At first glance, the taping of the doors makes you mad. "Who taped the doors?" you want to say. But wait a minute and look at the larger picture. This is a fully purposeful taping. They are taped to prevent them from opening due to the weight of the paper chain.*

For her project on horses, a student might include an area for other kids to jump over a cardboard roll held up by two chairs.

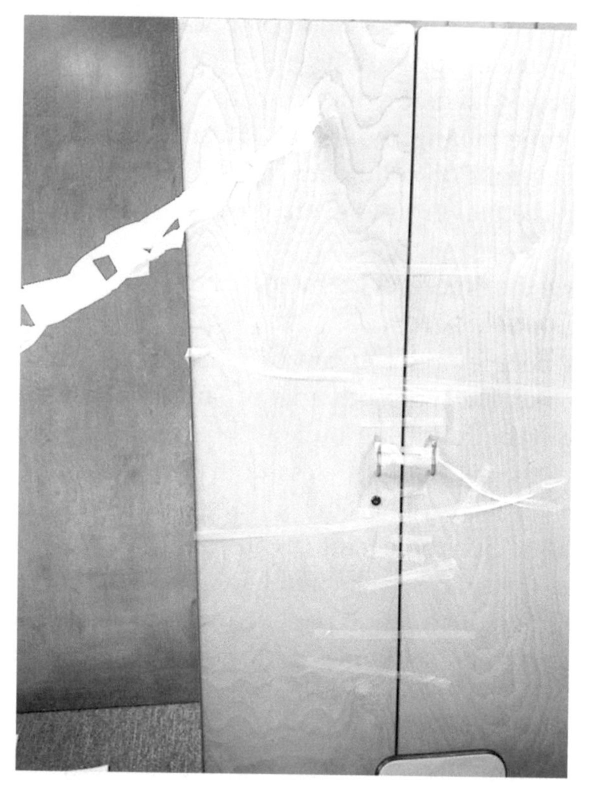

IMAGE 6.1
Example of authentic children's work in Heidi's classroom

A student prepared an area and included skeletal models of horses, research books, and a book she wrote with a partner. A teacher never would have thought to include horse jumps in a science center on horses, but horse jumping is something she knows about, has seen, or is interested in learning more about, plus it's fun!

Drawing and Writing Samples

The developmental writing process we shared in the Orange chapter is a wonderful way to showcase the growth of a young child's emergent writing. Collecting each piece of writing in a portfolio allows you to present the work as a piece of artwork that aims not to show perfection but PROCESS. If every piece of writing is presented perfectly, what is it teaching the reader about how children learn? The viewer then thinks that's how children actually write and learn. Perfectly edited pieces do no one any good in early childhood and it teaches children to dislike writing. Let the errors show; let their *work* show through. Do not be afraid to *share the actual work of the children*, no matter what *you* perceive the flaws to be! THAT is the process: an accurate documentation and reflection of learning.

Photographs

Many teachers take photographs of the RESULT of learning versus the PROCESS of learning. One of the many things to learn and study from inquiry-based programs and philosophies is an emphasis on the continued study of the process of documentation. While school policy and practice often ask teachers to use checklists or narratives to reflect children's skills in school, the inquiry method emphasizes documenting the process of learning. Photographs are a wonderful way to share the work of children. Most often when teachers take photographs, they show the adorable little kid proudly showing off their latest creation; however, the challenge of photographic documentation is for the teacher to focus on capturing the process of the work that is taking place. A practice suggested by Reggio Emilia philosophy is to put the camera in the hands of the children, which is an eye-opening reflection of the classroom for both teachers and students!

Movies and Video

Movies and video require a bit more planning (and bandwidth) to pull off, but are a powerful method of documenting learning. While scripted performance-type videos have their place, catching the spontaneous moment of a child actively engaged in problem-solving on video isn't easy.

Tips for utilizing videos and movies:

- Use one device for recording to minimize splicing and sharing videos across devices

- Film in one continuous motion, keeping as steady as you can
- For privacy reasons, avoid showing children's faces and instead focus on the work at hand. Film from directly above.
- Keep videos short (two minutes and under)
- Move videos to platforms such as Vimeo or YouTube, and protect them with the same password so you can limit sharing, but embed and share as needed.
- Remember, the goal is to show the process of learning versus a finished product or polished presentation
- Try having children make their own movies through Seesaw or other accessible platforms. (Just be careful as movies will eat up storage!)

Sharing and Celebrating Learning

Presentations, reflections, and celebrations of learning are a powerful and still underutilized tool. Setting a date for students to present their work and share their process of learning gives perimeters to your units and helps give structure to students and yourself! Whether you do this within your own classroom, for another class, parents, the wider school, or the town community, it is important to make the process of children's learning visible and accessible. We should all have the opportunity to see what a child is thinking at any age.

Showcasing and celebrating your work is as important for teachers as it is for kids. It's important both your communities know about some of the work you are doing in your classroom. Your class should host multiple public events per year. Yep, you heard that right! MULTIPLE PUBLIC EVENTS! That doesn't mean opening your classroom to the public; instead, it can mean:

- allowing children time to share their work and accomplishments with other classmates.
- performing a play or giving a presentation to parents.
- inviting members of your school community to an event.
- displaying class work at the public library.

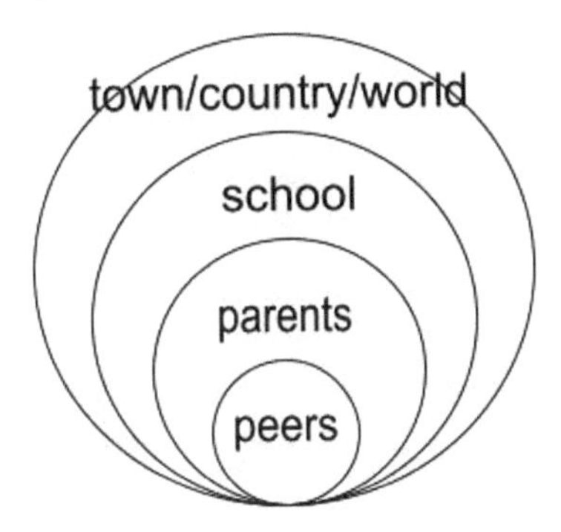

FIGURE 6.2
Spheres of sharing

Sharing doesn't always have to be a "show and tell" type of presentation. Sharing can be:

- a quick roundtable share-out with your class.
- 1:1 sharing.
- small-group share-outs.
- drawings detailing their plans.
- photographs.
- videos.
- portfolios.
- going for walks with adults in the school community.
- sharing with another class, peers, younger or older students.
- a celebration planned by your class for another class, grade, members of the school community, or parents.
- art shows, plays, and performances.
- game shows and movement shows.
- interactive events: cafés, museums, stores, factories, fairs.
- class-made gifts to leaders in the community, guests, and school staff.

Celebrating and sharing learning regularly and with different spheres of the whole community is a key component to every class, school, and program.

Reflection and Feedback

Report Cards

Report cards, aka every teacher's nightmare! In many cases, report cards have morphed into tomes of narrative written in single-spaced eight-point font. If you're lucky, your report card is a checklist of skills with a short section for comments. If you're even luckier, the comments are prewritten for you and you just indicate which one you'd like to add for Susie! Each of these approaches is extreme to some extent, and we have to constantly ask ourselves as educators, why am I doing this and what am I trying to communicate?

A report card most often functions as a formal record of a child's progress "toward grade-level goals." Who sets and decides those goals is a whole can of worms. A good question to ask is, "How does the accounting of how individual children measure up against grade-level benchmarks help us best serve individual children's needs?"

First, we need to agree on grade-level goals, which we won't argue here for the sake of brevity and sanity. While some countries like England have very strict (and we would say non-developmentally appropriate) standards in many cases, MOST accepted standards of grade-level goals are within the span of Developmentally Appropriate Practice. *(We have a fabulous collection of standards from around the world over at Kinderchat.org if you are looking to compare them, btw!)* Arbitrary aside, sets of short basic skills checklists are helpful to help you identify and record specific areas of weakness and strength in each child.

Often, report cards are trying to do too many things. Skills checklists serve as a more constant ongoing assessment rather than one or two times a year, and can be quick check-ins. Narratives describing each child's social, emotional, and academic growth and goals require more time, attention, and writing skill. These are the reports we write to serve as a snapshot of who the child is as a learner, friend, and human.

Any way your school decides to report, take a look at how far this area of early childhood has changed by reflecting on our friend Mardelle Sauerborn's (@learningmurd) kindergarten report card from 1971.

HAZEL M. KELLINGTON SCHOOL
Neepawa, Manitoba

KINDERGARTEN REPORT, JUNE 1971.

Name of student Mardelle Hunter

Comments:

Promoted to Grade One.

I expect Mardelle to make good progress with the Grade I course. She certainly hasn't had any difficulties in kindergarten and we have enjoyed having her.

Muriel Cherry
Signature of Teacher

IMAGE 6.2
Kindergarten report card from 1976

Other Types of Reporting and Feedback

As many schools move to more project-based and individual goal- and growth-based models, portfolios can become an essential piece of creating a portrait of a learner. However, portfolios can quickly become unwieldy and overwhelming. You need to know exactly where you are going when you choose this type of reporting! You can't be scrambling for "that project we did in January." You need to have collected pieces throughout the year and have been intentional about what you are collecting and showcasing. We give you the sequence of a writing portfolio in our "Year at a Glance" in the Orange chapter on the curriculum. Portfolios are a powerful tool of reporting and feedback and when done well, can form a cherished gift to families and children. That said, they can be extremely labor intensive if not approached intentionally and if done without enough time to regularly collect and assemble materials!

Feedback

Conferences, report cards, check-ins, and frequent e-mails and correspondence with children's caregivers are all important aspects of staying in conversation with caregivers about their children's development. Stop to think about how amazing it is that there's an entire workforce dedicated to each child's social, emotional, and academic well-being! That said, don't leave the CHILD out of this process! Children appreciate and NEED your feedback! Young children are busy, so keep it short, relevant, and targeted. Responding to certain behaviors in the moment is invaluable, while sharing a quiet moment of reflection with a child lets them know that you care about them, are aware of their strengths and challenges, and that you are there to support them as they grow.

Assessment Checklist: Academics and Social-Emotional Development

Math:

- Enjoys and engages in math activities
- Counts to 100
- Adds and subtracts numbers 1–5
- Accurately counts a number of objects under 20
- Identifies various symbols (math symbols, traffic signs, technology, trees/leaves)
- Demonstrates 1:1 correspondence

- Works cooperatively in teams
- Sorts objects and blocks by attribute
- Follows and creates sequences of steps

Reading:

- Enjoys reading and listening to books
- Identifies letters and sounds A–Z (by November or first reporting)
- Independently applies phonics to writing (by January)
- Writes in sentences (by end of year)
- Speaks clearly
- Rhymes words easily, accurately
- Claps in time to music
- Demonstrates grade-level fine motor skills (scissor work, handwriting, drawing)
- Demonstrates grade-level large motor skills (skips, balances, displays core strength)

Social-Emotional and Work Habits:

- Plays well with others
- Takes turns and cooperates with peers
- Handles frustration and disappointment age appropriately
- Adapts to transitions with ease
- Follows multistep directions
- Cleans up and helps in the classroom
- Is responsible for coat, jackets, lunchbox

References and Recommended Reading

Association of Montessori Internationale. (2020). *Biography of Maria Montessori*. www.montessori-ami.org/resource-library/facts/biography-maria-montessori.

Crockett, P., & Dunsiger, A. (2019–2020). *Mrs. Crockett & Mis Dunsiger's daily documentation*. https://oslerk.commons.hwdsb.on.ca/.

Echternacht, H. (2011–2020). *The treehouse*. https://kindergarden123.net/2014/10/03/welcome-fall-wait-whats-happening-out-there/
Kohn, A. (2005–2020). *Alfie Kohn: Blog posts*. www.alfiekohn.org/blog/.
Ontario Ministry of Education. (2016). *The Kindergarten Program*. www.ontario.ca/document/kindergarten-program-2016?_ga=2.84499417.1319520133.1608957844-166170227.1608957844.
Rinaldi, C. (2006). *In dialogue with Reggio Emilia*. Routledge.
Stager, G. (2013–2020). *CMK Futures*. cmkfutures.org.

7

Violet: Professional Life

Here's the thing about teaching: you could work 160 hours a week and still not feel like you are "done" with everything that can possibly be done. While this is true at any grade level, kindergarten adds the additional challenge of how physically exhausting it can be (who knew that your feet can hurt all the way up to your waist?). We all talk about meeting children's developmental needs, but it is just as important to take care of your own basic (and not-so-basic) needs, to avoid burnout, and to find laughter instead of tears on the craziest days.

The Policy and Politics of Teaching Young Children

Your Role in the Community

When we started Kinderchat, we came up with five goals. Along with facilitating discussions and highlighting different philosophies and practices, we felt one of our most important roles was "to promote real-life experiences of working with young children." We feel a responsibility not to paint the realities of childhood in a saccharine light, but to share honestly, authentically, and genuinely about the challenges, frustrations, rewards, and realities of working with young children.

Too often, children (and the elderly for that matter!) are invisible to our communities; they are to be "seen and not heard."

Having the beginning and ending periods of human life isolated and invisible harms society by taking away the essence of what it means to be human. The loudness, messiness, and rawness of children (and the elderly!) help us grow in compassion, understanding, wisdom, and the fullness and richness of life. YOU are part of the essential communication among children, their caregivers, policy makers, and society as a whole. The role of "teacher" brings hope to a community. Never forget that being "just a teacher" is actually a deep and complex role and responsibility.

Global Education

When Kinderchat formed in 2010, the far reaches of the Internet probably heard the squeals of delight as a group of adults quickly recognized each other's stories as people who spend A LOT of time with little kids. We also realized that it was 92 F in Texas and -20 C in Saskatchewan right at that same moment. Knowing temperatures differ and actually talking to someone sweating in shorts while you are bundled up and scraping ice off your windshield are different levels of experience. Our differences, similarities, locations, and circumstances instantly had more meaning and wonder as our worlds suddenly expanded from our individual locations. While that may all sound quaint in today's digitally connected world, at the time it was novel!

During those first few years we tried all kinds of different ways of connecting our classrooms. Collectively and individually, teachers designed a wide array of global projects, from the organized sign-up for buddies to chaotic-random projects where we zoomed into each other's classes spontaneously. We were teachers on the loose, trying new things and experimenting with technology. It was a ton of fun. We learned a bunch about what worked and what didn't and the successes and difficulties of globally connecting classrooms.

Through all of the challenges and fun of integrating global projects, the most effective project has been the #kinderchat meeting itself, where we have continued our weekly public meetings for now over ten years. Having the opportunity to network with a wide variety of educators helps you gain access to new perspectives, problems, and support systems that your district or school may or may not have. Networks offer the opportunity for colleagues to encounter a wider variety of educators and communities, which ultimately helps inform and improve your professional practice.

Unique Challenges of Working with Low-Income Students

Throughout this book we've tried to repeatedly make the case for the education of young children based on DAP and through inquiry and *active exchanges* between kids and teachers. It is unfair that children of wealth are allowed one standard of practice of education, and children of low economic status are dealt another. It is important that you as a professional recognize that while there are a number of factors that children in poverty face, one of the most glaring is the *freedom to play.*

Socioeconomic status affects *every aspect* of a child's and a family's life and cannot be underestimated in its importance and the weight it carries when thinking about society and the education of children. Frankly, nothing much in this book matters when little Josie doesn't have a home, food, clean clothes, and the basics she needs to succeed in school each day. Low socioeconomic status often brings undue chaos and complexity to families. You are in a primary role of providing support to your students. In many cases, teachers are functioning as social workers, helping identify children who need additional services and supports. Coordinating these services while delivering an entire educational program is extremely difficult, if not impossible. Low-income students especially need highly experienced teachers who can juggle these demands. Working together with your school community, families, government systems, and district supports is essential.

Addressing Issues of Equity and Bias in the Classroom

It has been well established that even the youngest of children face bias within the classroom. Education largely presents a view of the world through White versions of history, White teachers, and White characters in books, while Black, Indigenous, and Brown children's stories and histories are treated as "the other." Wealth and health are often presented as the default accepted standard of society, while issues of poverty or disability are hidden away or ignored. You as a professional must be constantly engaged in thinking and learning about bias and inequity in the classroom so that you can identify when it occurs and make moves to protect children who face unfair standards. For young children, using animal puppets is particularly effective in broaching issues of bias and equity for class discussion and helps foster greater compassion and understanding among young children.

Addressing the Needs of Children of Color

Every child has the right to see herself represented in her classroom and world. It should go without saying that your dolls, toys, educational materials, artwork, and crayons and colors represent a wide variety of skin colors and that every child can "see herself" not only in her classroom but also in the curriculum and program. Even if your school community isn't very diverse, children need to see that humans come in wide varieties of skin colors and cultures. Ensuring that the materials in your classroom are representative of a global community and not just a child's personal experience or hometown is one of the most important tools and opportunities you can provide your students. Thinking globally helps children gain a wider view of the world and helps children see themselves as part of a larger network of complex history, peoples, and cultures.

Additionally, it is of *paramount importance* that as part of your professional practice, you are constantly engaged in the work of anti-racism. It is not easy work to uncover and discover personal biases and it can be both frustrating and uncomfortable. Challenging yourself to read more, listen more, and experience more new music, movies, and art than you normally interact with can be an eye-opening adventure. Challenge yourself to constantly reflect on your curriculum and where you can improve representation or where you might need to learn more. Engaging in the practice of anti-racism is critical for every educator's unique role in the community.

Working and Playing With Others (and Hopefully Finding Your People)

As we said in the introduction, it has been our experience that kindergarten teachers can be at high risk of professional isolation. In many schools, there is only one kindergarten class, and it is considered so different from "real grades" that other teachers may not think they have much common ground with their early years colleagues. Working in isolation is not only lonely, but it will limit your ongoing professional and personal growth as an educator. It makes intuitive sense that if people need people, teachers need teachers. Where this gets challenging is finding fellow educators who make us better, as both human beings and professionals. We need people who will help us grow and stay connected to the joy of what we do. At #kinderchat, we refer to this as "finding your People," whether they are in your own classroom, across the hall, down the street, or across an ocean.

Sharing Your Classroom: The Arranged Marriages of Education

If you are lucky, you have another adult in your classroom for at least part of the day. These people can be your greatest assets and blessings, and at the same time, teaching with an audience can raise the bar and make you feel vulnerable. It's one thing to enthusiastically do the Hokey Pokey with 23 five-year-olds, and a whole other thing to Hokey-Pokey when another adult can see and hear you! Additionally, in most situations, you will not get to choose your classroom colleague(s). Hopefully, the match has been made by someone who knows and respects both of you, with consideration for your skills, backgrounds, and talents, but often, it is a matter of chance and convenience. There are two most common scenarios for this:

1. Team Teaching
   By "team teaching" we are referring to a model where there are two teachers present, engaged with students, at the same time. (This is different from job sharing, where two teachers share a classroom but teach at different

times). This can be a dream situation if you immediately "click" and have compatible teaching styles. It can also be very challenging if your styles are widely divergent.

2. Educational Assistants/Teaching Assistants/Aides/Paraprofessionals
   While these angels are becoming increasingly rare in public education, they are out there! Depending on your setting, their job title and associated responsibilities may vary, but if you have one of these people, they are an essential part of your classroom team. These partnerships work most effectively when they are partnerships, without a hierarchy of importance or authority. Typically, the "lead" teacher has some additional responsibilities that extend beyond the school day (report cards and parent communication are the two most common examples), but from the time the children arrive until they leave, you are partners in facilitating learning. The most powerful sign of an effective partnership is when the children perceive and believe that they simply have two teachers.

Whether you are team teaching or collaborating with a paraprofessional, here are a few tips to help things go smoothly:

- Make time to connect before the children arrive at the start of the school year. Sit down together and talk about what you each bring to the partnership. Speak candidly about:
  - your professional background and training.
  - the parts of teaching you love most.
  - the parts that are most difficult for you.
  - things you are really good at, and things you wish you could do better.
  - Your tolerance for:
    - noise.
    - clutter.
    - schedule changes.
  - your beliefs and practices about play.
  - any personal pet peeves or phobias.

- any allergies or health conditions that may be relevant while you are at school. (Your health is of course your personal business, but if you have a condition such as an anaphylactic allergy, it seems important for a close colleague to know about it!)
- any personal or family context that may be relevant to your job. (Again, no need to share things that are deeply private, but if you absolutely have to leave by 3:30 on Thursdays to take your own kiddo to soccer, this is helpful for your closest colleague to know.)
- classroom tasks that you find easy and enjoyable, as well as those that you find unpleasant.

- Make a schedule and divide up the work. It is much easier to plan this clearly and together than to just assume you have the same understanding of how things will go. Things to cover:
- Who does what, when.
- When A is doing ____, what is B doing?
- Do these tasks rotate or stay the same all week/month/year?
- When will you revisit this and see if adjustments are needed? (We recommend touching base after about 6–8 weeks.)
- Breaks – when are lunch/bathroom breaks for each of you?
- Rules/expectations about leaving the room (and communication when leaving)
- Roles and responsibilities in regard to:
  - instruction.
  - assessment.
  - planning.
  - parent communication and meetings.
  - supervision:
    - recess
    - snacks/meals
    - transitions
  - prep periods/specialist classes.
  - classroom cleanliness and organization.

- Communicate about communication:
  - Should parents include both of you in their e-mails?
  - How and when will you contact each other outside of school?
    - E-mail?
    - Text?
    - Phone call?
    - Any boundaries around this?
- Plan for when one of you is away. Some paraprofessionals are quite comfortable leading circle time while a substitute teacher looks on; others prefer to continue in their normal role, supporting the sub. Talk about this in advance, and capture it in your sub plans.

Outside of Your Classroom: Allies in Your Building

In an ideal world, every classroom full of young children would have at least two adults in the room, and those adults would sincerely value and enjoy one another's company. If this is not your reality (it really is very precious and rare), it is even more important to find at least one other person in your building that you connect with.

Beware the Staff Room!

The staff room/faculty lounge can be both a haven and a hazard. While it can be rejuvenating to have an "adults only" retreat away from small eyes and ears, pay close attention to the overall atmosphere in this den of coffee and laminator fumes.

Some schools have a staff room that really serves as a community hub for teachers. Everyone feels welcome, and there are treats on the table on Fridays. There are always listening ears and constructive feedback when someone shares a story about a worrisome student or a family in crisis. A staff room like this is a gift and a blessing; 15 minutes in here will sustain you through the rest of even the most exhausting kindergarten day!

In contrast, there are also staff rooms that can drain, rather than replenish, your energy and spirit. If most of the conversation involves "venting" about students, parents, workload, and admin, think carefully about whether this is the best atmosphere to refresh your spirit before the tiny humans return from recess.

Finding Your Allies

The staff room is not the only place to find your people in your own school building. While the very structure of a school day can make it hard to connect with other adults, there are some sneaky ways to gain insight into which colleagues might be a fit for your philosophy, values, and sense of humor:

- Notice the hallway bulletin boards: The choices that teachers make about how to use this valuable real estate can tell you a lot about their pedagogical approach and personality. If you notice boards that consistently feature unique, process-based student work (and NOT 25 identical owl crafts), that invite interaction and reflection, and that capture student voice and choice, take a minute to pop in, share a compliment, and say hello.
- Ask for help. If you teach kindergarten, and a worrisome student has a sibling in second grade, drop in on the second-grade teacher to ask about their experience with the family. Teachers who have been at a school for a long time will often remember when your kindergarten students were born, and will share tidbits of family history that can help you figure out your young learners. Even if a colleague is new to the school, they may have taught your grade level elsewhere, have specialized training in early numeracy, or have a previous career in special education. People love to be needed, and to share what they know.
- Reach out to newbies. Whether someone is new to the profession or to your building, everyone appreciates a friendly face. If you are new as well, how much nicer to be new together! If you are well established in your school community, be the voice of encouragement while you explore this new grade level.

Widening the Net: Finding Your People across the Street, or across the World

While hopefully you will connect well with at least one other teacher in your own building, we also strongly recommend that teachers connect with educators from other settings, as well. Seeing how other schools function, how another classroom manages routines, and how another country manages their school system will provide you with important reflection points about your own context and practice. Meeting other people who do the same work as you, in different settings, can help you find your voice in the large landscape of early education. It can also lead to authentic friendships and (as in our own case) partnerships on projects that cross international boundaries.

Men in Early Childhood Education

The early childhood sector of education is definitely dominated by women, but there are many men out there doing great work. It's especially important for young boys to have men to look up to as role models. In the classroom, men provide perspectives that are often missing from early childhood settings, especially when it comes to the importance of large motor movement and rough-and-tumble play. Most famous and not to be missed is longtime educational blogger Thomas Hobson, better known as "Teacher Tom." His blog and books provide wonderful reflective practice for early educators, both men and women.

Visiting Other Schools

This is one of the most straightforward ways to start building your network. Ask your principal or administrator if you can visit another school site. Some districts will provide release time for this (especially if it is part of a teacher's annual growth plan), and others may let you do so on a professional development day. If your school is not able to accommodate this, these visits can be powerful enough that they are worth giving up some personal time. If a nearby district has a slightly different calendar than yours, reach out directly to the principal of a school you would like to see, asking about a visit on a date when your own district is on a break.

Do not be afraid to visit schools that are of a different model than yours. If you teach in a public school, but are curious about a nearby charter, private, or parochial school, it is worth sending a courteous professional e-mail, asking about a possible visit.

Hosting Guests

As much as your administration will allow, make your classroom open to any and all visitors. If a colleague mentions a college-aged student who is interested in early education, let them know that you would welcome them as a guest observer. If you cross paths with another teacher at a bookstore, invite them in. It may be unnerving at first, but having guests in your classroom will help you be more aware of yourself as an educator, and word will start to spread that you are open to connecting with the larger field of early educators in your area.

Conferences and Workshops

Whenever you can, attend conferences, seminars, and workshops that include teachers from multiple schools and/or districts. While some of you may find it very comfortable, and even enjoyable, to socialize around the morning coffee and pastries, it is also perfectly OK to set a smaller goal of chatting and exchanging e-mail addresses with one new connection. As we talked about in the Yellow chapter, conferences for professions that are adjacent to education (psychology, social work, and so on) can be particularly rich environments for new professional connections and collaborations.

Connecting Online

Given our own history, we cannot help but advocate for leveraging social media as a place to find some of your People. As we write this in 2020, we, of course, are advocates for Twitter, but there are teacher communities to be found on nearly every social media platform. No matter which sites you use and prefer, we recommend the following:

- Observe for a while at first. Once you have found a group or hashtag that seems to be a fit for your context and philosophy, spend a little time lurking, to understand the tone, culture, and pace of what already exists there.

- If you are posting publicly and as yourself, only post or share content that you are comfortable with your principal and/or classroom parents seeing.
- Read, understand, and follow your school's or district's social media policies for teachers.
- Decide in advance if you are going to interact with colleagues online. If you choose to do so, be mindful of how much personal information your posts disclose.
- Do not engage with school families on social media. Use your school e-mail for school-related communication. If a parent messages you on another platform, respond from your school e-mail.
- Be cautious of the "edu-celebrity" culture. There are many consultants and companies that use education-related hashtags to promote their own services or products. Take the time to figure out who they are and where they stand to profit. Look for transparency and full disclosure of what these accounts may gain from any materials, books, or events that they promote.

Working With Volunteers

Good classroom volunteers are truly the Holy Grail of teaching. In addition to saving you time and labor, they also enrich your students' experience and help build strong connections between your classroom, students' families, and the larger community.

Before you go out recruiting, review your school's or district's policies, practices, and requirements around having volunteers in your classroom. In some settings, volunteers can help with non-instructional work only, or must be under the direct supervision (meaning line of sight) of a school staff member at all times. Some districts require that in-class volunteers sign a confidentiality agreement, to ensure they do not discuss students' behavior or performance with anyone. Make sure you know the rules and follow them, to protect yourself and your precious volunteers!

Finding Volunteers

While your students' parents are the most obvious source of volunteer help, they are not the only possibility. Other avenues to consider:

- parents from other grade levels, or parents of alumni
- grandparents, aunts, uncles, cousins, adult siblings of students
- your own friends and family members
- retired or partially retired community members
- postsecondary students (especially in programs related to education and/or child development)
- older students in your own school (many fifth graders are very happy to come spend their recess sharpening pencils or prepping craft materials!)

Things Volunteers Can Do to Help You

It is a strange reality that, while teachers are highly trained, educated professionals, we also do a great number of tasks that do not require any special skills or training. This is an introductory list. As you go about your daily routines, notice how many things you do that could easily be done by a volunteer! Many of these can be done at home and outside of school hours; many working parents are grateful to be able to contribute to the classroom without having to take time away from their jobs.

- prepare materials for lessons, activities, or art projects
- make Play-Doh
- organize classroom materials
- read to/with students
- facilitate a learning center:
  - play a card or board game with students
  - supervise an art or craft project
- reinforce basic skills:
  - letter names and sounds

  - number names and subitizing
  - scissor skills
  - sight words
- organize student work for portfolios
- update bulletin board or art wall
- take class laundry home to wash it
- wash classroom materials (at school or at home in their dishwasher)
- do light cleaning in the classroom
- sharpen pencils
- act as "guest speakers" and share their profession, culture, hobbies with the class

Balance and Boundaries As Professional Responsibilities

It is no secret that most teachers are deeply committed to their profession, and while this is one of our collective strengths, we would also argue that our profession has a self-care problem. The culture of education has evolved to glorify the teachers who work past dinner time every day, spend their summers in PD sessions, and start setting up their classrooms three full weeks before students arrive. While this model has become pervasive, it is our position that not only is it unrealistic, it is actually harmful: to individual teachers, to our profession as a whole, and to our students. A healthy, balanced teacher is a better teacher. Period.

Two essential truths:

1. Teaching is not a 24-7 gig.
2. You can be a great teacher without working 60-hour weeks.

Managing Your Work Hours

Teaching is a job where the work is never done. There is no magical moment when everything that you can possibly do is done, and you can head home with a clear to-do list. That moment does not exist, and the best thing you can do for yourself is to stop chasing that moment. There is no prize for working ten-hour days or 60-hour weeks. What's more, this job can be done without piling up unpaid overtime. Here's how to do it:

- Arrive early *or* stay late; don't do both.
  Most schools expect teachers to arrive 15–30 minutes before students, and to stay 15–30 minutes after dismissal. If you plan and prioritize carefully, it is entirely possible to do this job with just one additional hour of work on most school days. The first step is to decide whether coming in early or staying late will work better for you, your body, your sleep schedule, your family's needs. There are pros and cons to both models.
- Every single morning, no matter what:
  Even if you are an afternoon prepper, spend the ten minutes before your students walk in the door, getting yourself ready to welcome them. Use the bathroom if you need to. Fill up your water bottle, top up your coffee, or make a fresh cup of tea. Close your e-mail. Make sure the lights are on, and the window blinds are open. Right before you open the door, or collect your students from the playground, put a smile on your face.
- Every single afternoon, no matter what:
  As soon as students are dismissed, reset the room so it is ready for the students to arrive in the morning. Update your visual schedule, put your morning message on the board, and set out the activities that students will do as they walk in. Set the stage. Do it now. This will take about 15 minutes, and then, if you are a morning prepper, you can leave. This way, if you are delayed for any reason in

TABLE 7.1

Arriving early versus staying late: points to consider

Arriving early	*Staying late*
School is often very quiet/few interruptions.	Colleagues are often available for collaboration and/or advice.
Very clear deadline to work in – students will arrive when the bell rings!	Flexible; you can add a few minutes to finish up a task completely.

the morning, you can waltz in, turn on the lights, put a smile on your face, and be ready for the students. It also means that if, for any reason, you are absent the next day, your room is ready for whoever is taking over for you.

Routine for Morning Preppers:
Arrive at school 75 minutes before your students. Go straight to your classroom. Do not stop to chitchat with a colleague. If you have classroom neighbors who also come in early, let them know that you need this uninterrupted time to be ready for your day. When you arrive, your room is already set up for the day (because you did that yesterday!), which means you have time to do the following things, in this order:

- Do any prep work that is required for TODAY.
- Deal with your e-mail.
- Fill in your daily plan for one week from today. (If you can build this habit, you will always be planning one week ahead.)
- Do any prep work that is required for tomorrow.
- Work on ongoing projects like report cards or portfolios.

When your students arrive, you will be ready for the day, and all you need to do after school is reset the room.

Routine for Afternoon Preppers:
Once your students leave the room: STAY IN THERE (unless, of course, you have a staff meeting, in which case you should definitely go to the meeting). Do not go next door or across the hall or upstairs to rehash the day with a colleague. The venting and rehashing is not the best use of your time right now. Stay in your classroom and set a timer or alarm for 75 minutes after dismissal. During that time, do the following things, in this order:

- Reset the room, as described above
- Do any prep work that is required for TOMORROW.
- Deal with your e-mail.

- Fill in your daily plan for one week from tomorrow. (If you get into this habit, you will always be planning one week ahead, which gives you time to be flexible and accommodate.)
- Do any prep work for the day after tomorrow.
- Work on ongoing projects like report cards or portfolios.

When your timer goes off, STOP WORKING and start getting ready to go home. Unless you have a looming deadline (most often, report cards), do not bring work home with you. You have used your time well and are ready for tomorrow. All you need to do in the morning is get yourself ready to greet your students.

The Need for Chitchat

One of the realities of teaching young students is that you may find yourself starved for adult conversation. This feeling is real, as is the need for conversation and connection. This is what makes it so easy and tempting to spend your precious before/after school time chatting with colleagues, which then means your prep and planning are pushed into your evenings and weekends. Here are some ways to ensure you get some grown-up interaction, while still managing your work hours:

- Make a recess date. Agree to meet a colleague in your classroom (or theirs) for a quick catch-up while your students are outside.
- Lunchtime walk. Have a regular time to go for a walk with a close colleague. This also has the advantage of taking you out of the staff room (see our staff room warning, below!).
- Shared prep times. If you and a teacher buddy have a common prep time, use that for regular "collaboration." Meeting your need for productive adult interaction is an appropriate use of this time!

Creating Boundaries with Parents (and Sometimes, Colleagues)

For many parents of kindergarten students, this is the first time their child has been away from them for multiple consecutive hours. Especially if this is their oldest child, they are learning what it means to be the parent of a child who attends school and, guess what? YOU are their teacher in this, too! As a kindergarten teacher, you are teaching this family what they can reasonably ask of their child's educators, and setting up expectations and boundaries for all the teachers who welcome this family in the future. By looking after yourself, you are also looking after your colleagues at future grade levels!

One of the paradoxes of teaching is that our professional life deals with what is often the single most important element of parents' personal life. Parenting is a 24-7 job. Teaching is not. You can see how this reality creates potential conflict, but there are ways to manage it. (*Important note: the tips below are what work well for us in most circumstances; there are unusual and specific situations that justify making special exceptions.*)

Email Boundaries

In the first week of school, tell parents that you monitor your e-mail from 30 minutes before school to 60 minutes after school (if your school day is 8:30–3:30, this means e-mail is monitored 8:00–4:30, on school days), and will reply within one business day. (This means that an e-mail sent at 5 p.m. on the Friday before spring break will not get a response before 8:00 on the first day back.) Stick to it. If you are consistent and responsive within these boundaries, most parents will honor them.

If you are working on creating clearer boundaries for yourself, one of the most powerful things you can do is to take your school e-mail off your phone (or at least disable it on weekends). Forcing yourself to access it on a computer makes it far less tempting to just take "a quick peek" before bed or on Saturdays.

Cell Phone Boundaries

This one is short and simple: do not give parents your cell phone number. You are not on call to them. They can reach you by e-mail and landline phone during regular working hours. Do not use text messages to communicate with parents, either. You are not obligated to be constantly available and responsive.

If you find yourself in a situation where logistics require sharing your cell phone number with parents (the most common is a field trip where parents are accompanying groups of students in a wide area like a zoo), answer their calls *for that event only*. After that, let their calls go to voicemail, and then respond via your school e-mail, during regular hours. Do the same thing for text messages; ignore the message when it is sent, and respond via e-mail during school hours.

All of the above points apply to colleagues as well. If you have already established a precedent of being constantly available to colleagues, you can ask for their help to get back on track: Gently tell them that you are working on work–life balance, and would be grateful if they kept the school questions to school hours.

Taking Care of Yourself

We have all heard the cliché about putting on your own oxygen mask before you help others. While this is true in times of crisis, we would argue that it is even more important to avoid getting into situations where "oxygen" is required.

You Are More Than Your Job

In a job where the work is truly never done, it is critical to see yourself as more than "teacher." Who are you when you are not "Miss So-and-so" or "Mr. Teacher-Man"? As hard as it can be, especially in the early years of your career, it is critical to have an identity outside of your classroom and school. Do you play an instrument, love movies, climb mountains? Are you a runner, a swimmer, a dancer, an artist, a reader? KEEP DOING THOSE THINGS. Make time for all the parts of yourself. Doing so actually makes you a better teacher! Some adults become so enmeshed in their identity as an educator that they lose track of themselves. While pop culture and mainstream media often glorify the teacher-as-martyr trope, the best teacher is a healthy, stable teacher.

Making the Most of Downtime

Whether it is a 15-minute recess on a crazy Monday, or those glorious weeks of summer break, you should not feel guilty for enjoying making the most of your time off.

During the School Day

Navigating and leading a class full of young children all day can be as intense as any Wall Street trading floor, and it's important you maximize any precious minutes of head space so you can stay calm, composed, and get back out there. A few tips:

- Use playground duty as a time to reflect, observe, breathe deeply and appreciate nature around you.
- If you can, take a walk at lunch or break times.
- Vary your lunch routine; alternate lunch with colleagues or your class.
- Go the long way on a school errand.
- Find a quiet or unused space to "hide out" on a break time.
- Keep a routine and strategy for dealing with e-mails and phone calls.
- Don't be afraid to model stopping and taking a nice, long deep breath when you need one!
- Play classical, jazz, or contemporary music. It can pull you out of a minute and help activate your imagination.
- Don't be afraid to tell children you "are closed for a few minutes" to hearing their problems, issues, wants, and needs. Sometimes they need to wait, and that's not a bad thing.

Protecting Your Weekends

Especially early in your career, it is easy to let your teaching work take over your weekends. If you have followed our advice throughout this chapter, you should be much closer to reclaiming your Saturdays and Sundays, but here are a few more suggestions:

- Stay late at school on Fridays. Yes, this seems counter-intuitive, but if it lets you take the rest of the weekend off because you feel ready for Monday, it is worth it.

- Set a time limit. If you have to get some planning done, commit to a day and a specific time frame (no more than two hours), and set a timer if you need to.
- Log out of your school e-mail when you leave on Friday. Don't touch it again until Monday morning.
- Make firm, committed plans for one social or recreational activity every weekend. Whether it is with your family, a friend, or on your own, do something that will bring you pleasure and connect you to the non-teacher parts of yourself.

Celebrating Vacation Time

There is no shame in admitting that having several long (and often one very long) breaks throughout the year is one of the perks of this profession. Do not be fooled by the teacher-martyr culture that says you should leverage this time to be even more ready to return to the classroom. Take this time as the gift it is.

- Put your "out-of-office" on your school e-mail. If needed, commit to checking for urgent messages mid-break, but no more than that.
- Limit your summer PD. There are some amazing teacher conferences offered in July and August, but do not let these consume your entire vacation. Choose **one** workshop, course, conference, or seminar.
- Consider your professional reading carefully. If there is a new pedagogical book (or several) that you are dying to read, commit to balancing it with pleasure reads at a 1:1 page ratio.
- Plan a mid-break one-day planning session. Doing this in the middle of your break will give you the peace of mind of knowing you are somewhat prepared to return to school, while still leaving you with some time off to enjoy before doing so.
- Get out of town at the start of your break. If there is any way to fit it into your budget, get a complete change of scenery for at least a couple of nights. A campsite or a motel in the next town, or even a short stay in your best

friend's guest room will help your brain disconnect from school, and provides a quick "reset" on your routines and mindset.

- Have a plan for the last day(s) of your break. Intentionally plan to do something fun to make the most of the last day or weekend before you return to school. This sets you up to feel like you made the most of your time and did not let it slip away from you.

Knowing When You Need Time Off

Inevitably, there will be a day when you are in no shape to be in the classroom. Whether you have come down with a flu, have injured yourself, have a sick family member, or have experienced a loss or other trauma, it is of critical importance that you recognize when you are not well or strong enough to teach. Taking a sick day (or a mental health day) is not a moral failure on your part. Perfect attendance is not an imperative for teachers (nor should it be for students). As we write this in the final weeks of 2020, it is our hope that one of the lasting lessons of the COVID-19 pandemic will be the importance of all of us staying home when we are not well. If you have followed the rest of our advice so far, your relationships and routines will carry your students through until you are well enough to return to work, whether that is in a day, a week, or a month.

Finally, we hope this book, this "Guide to the Classroom" serves as a companion to you when you are tired and feel you have none. Know that throughout the world there are teachers of young children doing the work and feeling the same weights, joys, pressures, and challenges you are feeling each day. You are never alone. You are not "just a teacher." It is YOU who are growing and sowing the seeds of peace and the freedoms of tomorrow.

References and Recommended Reading

Brazas, C., & McGeehan, C. (2020). *What white colleagues need to understand: White supremacy doesn't stop at the teachers' lounge door.* www.tolerance.org/magazine/spring-2020/what-white-colleagues-need-to-understand.

Chiarello, E. (2012). *Social justice: The Teaching Tolerance Anti-Bias Standards.* [PDF File]. www.tolerance.org/sites/default/files/2017-06/TT_Social_Justice_Standards_0.pdf.

Derman-Sparks, L., & Olsen Edwards, J. (2009). *Anti-bias education for young children and ourselves.* National Association for the Education of Young Children (NAEYC).

Hobson, T. (2017). *Teacher Tom's first book: Teaching and learning from preschoolers*. Peanut Butter Publishing

Hobson, T. (2020). *Teacher Tom's second book: Teaching and learning from preschoolers.* Peanut Butter Publishing.

Hobson, T. (2000–2020). *Teacher Tom: Teaching and learning from preschoolers*. http://teachertomsblog.blogspot.com/.

Jewell, T. (2020). *This book is anti-racist: 20 lessons on how to wake up, take action, and do the work.* Frances Lincoln Children's Books.

Lemon, D. (2020, July 2). *Silence is not an option: schooling the system. [Audio Podcast]. https://omny.fm/shows/silence-is-not-an-option/schooling-the-system.*

Appendix

Year-At-A-Glance Digital Download

Math and Science

Month	*Goals/Structure*	*Lessons and Skills*	*Projects*	*Play/Explore*	*Teamwork Tables*	*Skill Supports*	*Presentations*
September	Establish balanced math community of inquiry, exploration, and skill work Apply code reading work from Ride and Read	Directionality Mathematical and computer tech symbols Slowly introduce varieties of math manipulatives one at a time	Begin to explore various math manipulatives at tables Begin to establish inquiry thinking and wonderings	Block center, cars, and road signs	Math manipulatives exploration (teams share their discoveries, projects at the end of each session)	Whole=group counting practice 1–100 Whole-group music and movement	Teacher: "I noticed," "what do you wonder"? Student: short share outs and reports
October	Individual skill assessments Introduce group rotation stations for skill work Continue ongoing promoting culture of inquiry, documentation, and share outs	Geometry: fractals, shapes,distinguishing features Attributes: sort and classify (leaves/trees nature)	Manipulatives exploration at tables, continue developing inquiry thinking **Tree study (begin year-long inquiry project)**	3D Blocks: build/ map the school or classroom	Teamwork Tables explore manipulatives, targeted skill work, and develop projects Block constructions: draw, label, and document designs	Launch Skill Centers: skills targeted through individual assessment Sort and classify (blocks, leaves) Matching set numbers of objects and numerical cards Shape matching	Teams or individuals share designs and present constructions, inventions Teams present findings, data, and next questions
November	Focus on group dynamics and cooperative learning Working with money Taking Apart and Putting Together 1–5	Money Addition and subtraction to 5 and 10	Author's Café	Brownie's Bank Author's Café: Making Change within 5 and 10	Play Author's Café and Brownie's Bank; working together to solve problems, team cooperation, leadership	Skill Centers; Pennies and nickels Adding and subtracting with pennies and nickels	Working as a team to operate a functional café

Month	Goals/Structure	Lessons and Skills	Projects	Play/Explore	Teamwork Tables	Skill Supports	Presentations
December	Express sequences in written form Math vocabulary	Sequencing, computing, and design thinking Interpreting steps and sequences	Prototypes and design for crafts and toys Cooking Origami	Toy Town: the designing and building of toys	Toy Town: partners, teams, or individuals design and build a prototype for a toy, record steps in written form for reproduction	Skill Centers: Sequencing sets of numbers; ordinal numbers	Dot and dash/Bee Bot robot/toy/Lego show "How To" videos, books, and instructions
January	Data and documentation: integrating science Games and Number lines	Keeping "track of" and scoring: recording, graphing, representing data Base 10 Moving on number lines	Weekly science centers Recording data Developing games on number lines	"The Lab": weekly rotating lab "kits": magnets, sink and float, create potions (What sinks? floats? What does this magnet stick to or not?)	Teams rotate through skill support centers and working at "The Lab"	Dice, card games, and moving back and forth on a number line Individual assessments	Students report findings to the class; record data; whole-class discussions Whole-group discussions of data from work in weekly science labs, record and share findings
February	Games and Number Lines Spatial language and directional words: under, through, inside, across, between Fact fluency 1–10	Sequencing, Symbols, and Subitizing Following and writing sets of patterns and directions	How many Xs can you do in a minute How many is two sets of ten? Develop sequences and repeating patterns	Workout World Obstacle courses (Kindergarten Ninja Warriors) Music and Dance studios	Cooperative game play: moving on a number line, dice and card games Teams develop routines for other teams to follow, teach patterns, dances, directional words	1:1 correspondence work Interpreting directional words, motions, and symbols Fact fluency 5–10 Targeted supports	Share-outs of progress/ issues in play centers Model and highlight mathematical discussions happening in Table Teams

March	Sort and classify: identifying attributes and patterns Rhyme, chant and rhythm Story problem solving	Attributes and sorting Counting by 2s, 5s, 10s	Surveys and graphing Classifying sets of objects, sorting boxes, sorting manipulatives, toys	Math Museums Math dances Sorting and organizing, creating, and curating collections	Dance and number chants Create/curate collections Collaborative problem-solving of story problems	Counting by 1s, 5s and 10s to 100 Labeling attributes Targeted supports	Team dances and math number chants Showcasing collections Sharing survey data Sharing story problem strategies
April	Number stories, logic, and strategy	Number Operations and Equations Algebraic thinking Addition and Subtraction to 10	Student demonstrates an integrated math component to literacy nonfiction project	Game centers: tic-tac-toe tournament developing and playing math strategy games	Working to collaborate and solve workbook/ written problems in teams; arrive at consensus	Tic-tac-toe tournament Independent/ Partner work on nonfiction project Targeted supports	Partner Projects Showcase: nonfiction centers from literacy
May	Individual skill assessment and reporting Center work	Proportion, scale, and measurement	Water table and mud kitchen	Woody's Woodshop Sanding sticks, building and construction, nails, sawing, measuring tapes, units of nonstandard measurement	Puzzles Drawing diagrams, maps, and planning final blocks presentation Teams working independently in math workbooks and problem-solving	Final individual assessments	Final presentation: Block representation of the classroom and school utilizing maps, diagrams, symbols, and directional language

Social studies and science are integrated throughout math and literacy month-by-month Year-At-A-Glance

Month	*Goals/Structure*	*Reading*	*Writing*	*Play*	*Speaking/ Listening*	*Skill Supports*	*Tech Integration*
September *3 weeks +/-*	Establish Ride and Read: • Motion cards • Extend time, techniques with 1:1 books	Road signs Motion cards **Fiction:** Wordless books Add Caldecott	Drawing and telling Cut and paste Stencils	**Outside play** Walks looking for environmental print **Personal responsibility and the Common Good:** *Clean up and peacemaking*	Partner sharing Wordless book read alouds Sharing drawn stories	Whole group clap games Alphabet and alphabetical order First names Tracing with stencils	Voice recordings of stories (voicethread, etc.) Kinderchat Digi Classroom
October *2–3 weeks*	Ride and Read: • Add bins Rotation stations for Word Work "Teacher-Kid" partner work	**Nonfiction:** Add Label books Bins: • Wordless • Caldecott • Label	Handwriting Work to independently add labels to drawings applying phonics skill work	Begin to open classroom centers **Outside play:** *Trees and leaves* **People in Our Neighborhood**	Morning class meetings Show n' share Phonics work	Sound and Motion Alphabet cards First/Last names Matching cards Handwriting	Label drawings (popplet)
November *3-week project*	Whole Group Read-alouds and performances Table Bins Rotation Stations/ Centers Partner read	**Fiction:** Author study: Bins: • Wordless • Caldecott • Label • Author bin	Handwriting Continue labeling drawings, apply sight words Cut-and-Paste project, illustration project	**Restaurant: Museum and Café** Server and chef trainings (self-reg.)	**Story plays** Chant, rhyme	Assess phonics; identify those who need additional skill practice Matching cards, fine motor centers Rhyming Rotation stations for targeted skill work	Teacher **documentation** of process through photographs and movie making

SUPPORT MATERIAL

December *3 weeks*	Whole group writing, reading small group crafting, making	**Nonfiction:** "How To" craft and recipe books, Lego instructions, origami directions, etc.	**How To Writing:** 1-, 2-, 3-step instructions through draw and label Sequence boxes	**STEM integration:** **"Toy Town"**: Crafting and makerspace centers	Morning class meetings, show n' share Share plans for makerspace toys	Sequence cards Add craft centers, sequencing work, and sensory bins to rotation stations	Use or create simple video instructions for origami, crafting
January	New routines and structures Whole-group read-alouds Add targeted work stations and 1:1 conferencing with leveled readers Introduce formal partner reading	**Fiction:** Character study **Easy/Leveled Readers:** For fluency, small group, partner reading, 1:1 reading	Handwriting **Dialogue:** Making characters talk using talking bubbles	**Bird study** **Weekly Science Center "Lab Kits"** **Community helpers**: *dress up, hats, puppets*	Morning meeting Show n' share Read writing out loud to three people Choral partner reading	Sight words Beginnings and endings of words, digraphs Intro Word Wall	Puppet Pals, Supporting phonics apps, integrated tech center
February *2–3 week project*	Whole-group read-alouds Targeted work stations and 1:1 conferencing with leveled readers Small-group "book clubs " that function as theater groups	**Fiction:** Stoplight Stories* Green: Go! Tell the Title, Author, and who is playing which Character Yellow: Slow Down! Tell the story. Look for patterns. Red: Stop and Think! What was this story trying to teach kids?	Sequence story boxes Incorporate and apply speech bubbles	**Weekly Science Lab "Kits"** **Fairy Tale Theater** Scaffold each fairy tale in slowly, mix up groups to perform each, then specialize and they present the work <u>Sample Program</u> **STEM integration: Costume and Set Construction**	Theater Plays: dynamic speaking, improv, social dynamics	Sequencing work: first, middle, last, after, before Sight words Blends and digraphs	Video documentation, create movies of fairy tales Storytelling apps Open listening center

Month	*Goals/Structure*	*Reading*	*Writing*	*Play*	*Speaking/ Listening*	*Skill Supports*	*Tech Integration*
March *2 weeks: Poetry*	Targeted work stations, 1:1 conferencing with leveled readers Individual writing projects	**Poetry:** Penny for a Poem*	Copying – make the transition to lined paper	**Fairy Tale Theater** Sensory centers, classroom centers	Memorize poem, chant, go on tour	Handwriting and printing on lines	Recording and play back for fluency checks Listening center, Add music, rhythm beat to nursery rhymes
April *Nonfiction* *2 weeks: Biography* *3–4 week Partner Inquiry and Research project*	Model reading for research writing Individual writing project (biography) Partner writing research project Targeted skill work stations, 1:1 time with teacher	**Nonfiction:** Biography: Famous Folks Research Project: Wide variety of texts as needed	Individual research project Biography: answer basic who, what, where, when, why, how Research project: planning webs, full written reports (2 pages each)	**Outside Ladybug Library** **STEM integration:** nonfiction final project presentation	Present biography to class, visitors. Kids can dress as person Presenting research project (science integration)	Basic sentence structure Applying sight words Translating questions to statements	Voki for biographies Popplet for inquiry presentations
May/June	Read-alouds and conversations Targeted skill work stations, 1:1 time with teacher Partner reading	Feelings unit	Feelings book Bind final portfolio of writing work	**Woody's Woodshop**: sanding and paper making **Move Outside**, slowly close up centers for summer	Puppets	Vowel work Site words Independent assessments and reports	Final writing portfolio presentation (on paper or integrated with tech)